At Issue

| Disposal of the Dead

Mater Dei Catholic High School
1615 Mater Dei Drive
Chula Vista, CA 91913

Other Books in the At Issue Series:

Can Celebrities Change the World?

Disaster Recovery Plans

Does the World Hate the U.S.?

Genetically Modified Food

Greenhouse Gases

Has Technology Increased Learning?

How Safe Is America's Infrastructure?

The Olympics

Polygamy

Should the U.S. Do Business with China?

Teen Smoking

The U.S. Policy on Cuba

What Is the Future of the Music Industry?

What Is the Impact of E-Waste?

What Is the Impact of Tourism?

At Issue

Disposal of the Dead

Diane Andrews Henningfield, Book Editor

GREENHAVEN PRESS
A part of Gale, Cengage Learning

Detroit • New York • San Francisco • New Haven, Conn • Waterville, Maine • London

Christine Nasso, *Publisher*
Elizabeth Des Chenes, *Managing Editor*

© 2009 Greenhaven Press, a part of Gale, Cengage Learning.

Gale and Greenhaven Press are registered trademarks used herein under license.

For more information, contact:
Greenhaven Press
27500 Drake Rd.
Farmington Hills, MI 48331-3535
Or you can visit our Internet site at gale.cengage.com

For product information and technology assistance, contact us at

Gale Customer Support, 1-800-877-4253
For permission to use material from this text or product, submit all requests online at www.cengage.com/permissions

Further permissions questions can be emailed to permissionrequest@cengage.com

Articles in Greenhaven Press anthologies are often edited for length to meet page requirements. In addition, original titles of these works are changed to clearly present the main thesis and to explicitly indicate the author's opinion. Every effort is made to ensure that Greenhaven Press accurately reflects the original intent of the authors. Every effort has been made to trace the owners of copyrighted material.

Cover image © Images.com/Corbis

LIBRARY OF CONGRESS CATALOGING-IN-PUBLICATION DATA

Disposal of the dead / Diane Andrews Henningfield, editor.
p. cm. -- (At issue)
  Includes bibliographical references and index.
  ISBN 978-0-7377-4092-9 (hardcover)
  ISBN 978-0-7377-4093-6 (pbk.)
  1. Funeral rites and ceremonies--Juvenile literature. 2. Burial--Juvenile literature.
I. Henningfield, Diane Andrews.
  GT3150.D57 2009
  393'.9--dc22

                                                                2008020843

Printed in the United States of America
1 2 3 4 5 6 7 13 12 11 10 09

Contents

Introduction   7

1. Disposal of the Dead Across Cultures   11
   Ealing Schools Service

2. The Dead Should Be Buried   23
   Michael Cahill

3. Burying the Dead Pollutes Groundwater   29
   Richard D.L. Fulton

4. Burials Can Be Environmentally Friendly   35
   Kirsten Scharnberg

5. Cremation Harms the Environment   42
   DeeDee Correll

6. Modern Crematories Are
   Environmentally Friendly   47
   Paul F. Rahill

7. Contemporary Funerals Honor the Dead   53
   Robert Kastenbaum

8. Contemporary Funerals Do Not
   Adequately Honor the Dead   65
   John Fraser

9. Contemporary Funerals Should Include
   the Body   75
   Thomas Lynch

10. Excarnation Is an Important   85
    Religious Tradition
    Rachel Laribee

11. Excarnation Is No Longer a Viable Way   90
    to Dispose of the Dead
    Braden Reddall

12. Plastination Is an Appropriate Way to   95
    Dispose of the Dead
    Tony Walter

Organizations to Contact   105
Bibliography   110
Index   114

Introduction

Across time and around the world, virtually every human culture has developed religious beliefs, rites, and rituals concerning death, including how dead bodies should be handled and ultimately disposed of. Hinduism, for example, requires that the dead be cremated, while Judaism stipulates that the dead should be buried. Even secular societies have developed methods for the disposition of the dead that honor the dead and help the living. As Dawn Rolke writes in a 2004 *Briarpatch* article, "The Rituals and Politics of Death," "In every known human society, rituals of death occupy a central and sacred place. . . . Rituals of death, like other life passage rites, reflect the culture in which they take shape."

What is now considered a "traditional" funeral in the United States and Canada is a relatively recent custom. During the American Civil War, the families of soldiers slain in battle wanted their sons returned home for burial. As Stephen F. Christy writes in the Spring 2007 issue of the *Land Trust Alliance Exchange*, "If Johnny couldn't come marching home, how still to get him back to his loved ones without making everyone sick?" Because bodies decompose quickly, it was necessary to develop embalming techniques that would preserve bodies long enough to get them home.

The custom of using undertakers and embalmers to handle the "laying out" of the body, previously handled by family members, grew in popularity through the end of the nineteenth century and continues to the present day. Today, most Americans and Canadians call a funeral director immediately upon the death of a loved one. The funeral director handles the entire process of disposing of the dead, from pickup at home or hospital to burial or cremation.

While this remains a standard procedure, many are beginning to question the environmental wisdom, as well as the expense, of contemporary funerary customs. As Peter Holder-ness writes in "A Movement for Green Life After Death," published in 2007, "Americans bury the equivalent of the Golden Gate Bridge every year in placing loved ones in cemeteries." He notes that environmentalists worry about the "environmental damage caused by the industrial burial of so much metal and the potential contamination from the 800,000 gallons of formaldehyde-based embalming fluids used each year."

These concerns have led to the growth of the "green burial" movement. In a green burial, the body is not embalmed, clothed in a simple, biodegradable shroud, then placed in a cardboard or wood box, then buried in either a certified "green" cemetery or on property owned by the family. By so doing, the body is able to decompose naturally, its elements returned to the earth without danger of contamination.

Just as the green burial movement returns to practices that were common in earlier times, another movement has returned to traditional ways of caring for the dead. Families choose to take care of their own dead rather than using the services of a funeral home and return to an earlier day where "Grandma would be propped up in the corner of the parlor for a day or two while folks came and said goodbye," as Christy describes it. Sometimes called the do-it-yourself funeral or home burial movement, the practice requires family and friends to undertake all of the tasks that are usually handled by a funeral home, including transporting, washing, clothing, and burying (or burning) the body. The idea of returning to the old customs was popularly introduced by Lisa Carlson in her book *Caring for the Dead—Your Final Act of Love* and has become an important part of the green burial concept. (Mark Harris, in his book *Grave Matters*, also reminds readers that "members of the Jewish burial society known as the Chevra Kadisha continue [the tradition of] washing their dead and covering the remains with a white cloth prior to burial, a practice similar to that observed by Muslims.")

Many people are surprised to learn that do-it-yourself funerals (including at-home viewing) are not only possible, but also legal in nearly every state. Anthony Gottschlich, in a 2007 article in the *Dayton* (Ohio) *Daily News*, outlines some of the steps, including reporting the death to the authorities if the person has not died in a hospital or nursing home; obtaining a death certificate; and obtaining a burial certificate. Beyond the legal matters involved with a home funeral, there are other important tasks the family or friends must accomplish. Workshops run by people such as Beth Knox and her Maryland nonprofit organization, Crossings, teach people what they must do to care for their dead. Harris describes Knox's workshop, and her reassurances to attendees that "remains don't break down immediately upon death, but noticeable effects of disintegration, such as leaking body fluids and odors will eventually occur if no steps are taken to retard decomposition." Knox and other home-burial experts recommend that after washing and dressing the body, death caregivers should place wrapped blocks of dry ice on and around the corpse. According to Harris, "With daily changes of dry ice, a body can be laid out for several days. In Beth [Knox's] experience, the traditional three-day wake works well for the purposes of the home funeral."

Another woman who helps arrange home burials is Jerrigrace Lyons, of Sebastapol, California. Bill Strubbe, writing in the April 2007 issue of *Common Ground*, describes Lyons's death midwifery practice. According to Strubbe, death midwives "assist with the paperwork [and] facilitate the transport and care of the body for a home ritual or wake."

What motivates families or friends to opt for a home burial or home funeral? Certainly a home funeral is much less expensive than a standard funeral home service. However, most people undertake the rigors of caring for their own dead for more spiritual or altruistic reasons. According to Lyons, as quoted by Strubbe, "The baby boomers are seeking personal and meaningful death rituals and ceremonies much like the home wedding, home birth and home schooling movements . . . Part of the boomers' legacy is reclaiming sacred rituals, bringing family and community together to participate in one of life's most important rites of passage."

Clearly, religion, culture, and environmental concerns all play a role in the disposal of the dead. The viewpoints that follow in *At Issue: Disposal of the Dead* demonstrate the many opinions regarding the proper disposition of human bodies after death and detail the many available options.

Disposal of the Dead Across Cultures

Ealing Schools Service

Ealing Schools Service supervises all schools in the Ealing borough of London, England. The service produces the Ealing Grid for Learning, a Web site providing curricular materials and faculty training, among other items.

People around the world have many different customs and traditions concerning the disposal of the dead. Most of these grow out of religious convictions. Hindus, for example, cremate the dead as do Sikhs. Muslims and Jews both have religious rites including the preparation and burial of the dead. Christians have traditionally buried their dead, but increasingly, many Christians are choosing cremation. Humanists, a group that does not hold religious convictions or belief in an afterlife, support burial, cremation, or other forms of disposal as desired by the individual.

Responses to death and the rituals and beliefs surrounding it tend to vary widely across the world. In all societies, however, whether customs prescribe overt displays of grief or restrained behaviour, the issue of death brings into focus certain fundamental cultural values. The various rituals and ceremonies that are performed are primarily concerned with the explanation, validation and integration of a people's view of the world. . . .

Hindu Cremation

Hindus believe in the law of karma which states that each individual passes through a series of lives until, depending on

Ealing Schools Service, "Funeral Rites Across Cultures," *Ealing Grid For Learning*, July 26, 2006. www.egfl.org. Reproduced by permission.

the actions of previous existences, the state of *moksha*, or liberation from the cycle of birth and rebirth, is attained. Consequently, death is not understood to be the end of a process, but is merely a stage in the long chain of transition. It is this continuity, extending beyond the limits of any single lifetime, which is enhanced and focused during the elaborate mortuary rituals performed by Hindus. The funeral ceremonies involve not only the immediate family members of the deceased, but also those of the extended kin network. Particular categories of kin have special ritual and economic duties to perform on this occasion. There are many regional and sub-cultural variations in the content and duration of mourning practices; the following is limited to describing the ceremonies in the broadest terms.

When death is imminent, the person is lifted from the bed to the floor so that the soul's free passage into the next life is not obstructed. Water from the holy River Ganges [in India] is given to the dying person and a *tulsi* (basil) leaf is placed in the deceased person's mouth. The *tulsi* leaf has a dual significance. Firstly, it is associated with Lord Vishnu, one of the three gods who are collectively known as the Hindu Trinity of gods; Vishnu is also known as the preserver of the universe. Secondly, the *tulsi* leaf is believed to have many medical properties.

The customary mode of disposal of a dead body amongst Hindus is by cremation.

After death, the body is washed and dressed, preferably in new clothes. Married women are clothed in a pink or red sari and adorned with jewellery. *Kumkum* red powder is placed in the parting of the hair and a red spot or *tilak* is applied on the forehead. The woman's father or brother usually provides the clothes, and when a man dies, the clothes are again provided by the wife's father or brother. . . .

Except for young children under one year of age who may be buried, the customary mode of disposal of a dead body amongst Hindus is by cremation. In the villages in India, the body is placed on a bier made of bamboo poles and carried on the shoulders of close male relatives to the burning grounds. In most cases, all the relatives in the village attend the cremation. The actual size of the gathering of mourners varies with the age and importance of the deceased. Thus, when an elderly and highly respected man dies, even his genealogically and geographically distant family would make it a point to attend the cremation. . . .

There are now electric crematoria in many cities in India, including one near the bank of the River Ganges in Varanasi. At cremation grounds, or *ghats*, the body is placed on a pyre of wood with the head pointing north in the direction of Mount Kailasha in the Himalayas. In the case of affluent families the wood of the pyre may be an expensive variety such as sandalwood. "Ghee" or clarified butter, is poured on the pyre to help it burn, and the pyre is then set alight by a son, brother or brother's son (in this order of priority). Other mourners will then throw fruit, flowers, incense and fragrant spices into the fire. Mourners traditionally attend the entire cremation, i.e. until the body has been totally consumed by the fire. In the final stages of this long process, the chief mourner (i.e. the male relative who first lit the pyre) breaks the skull with a long pole in order to allow the soul to escape, a rite known as *kapol kriya*. On the fourth day (in certain parts of India this may take place on the third day), the ashes are collected by the chief mourner and the place of cremation cleared. The ashes are then traditionally immersed in a river, preferably the Ganges. Any items of jewellery that have not melted in the fire are collected and distributed among the mourners, along with a simple meal, usually a food called *kitcheree*, a mixture of boiled rice and lentils. . . .

Sikh Cremation

Sikhs believe that birth into the faith is a result of good "karma." Death is the door to union with God.

The cremation is a family occasion attended, as far as possible, by the close relatives of the deceased and friends.

If the deceased was the head of the family, the oldest son is given a turban to symbolise the taking on of responsibility for the family.

Prior to the funeral the body is washed and clothed by members of the family. The dead person is attired with the symbols of the faith known as the 5Ks—*Kesh* (uncut hair), *Kanga* (comb), *Kara* (steel bangle), *Kachs* (shorts) and *Kirpan* (short sword)—and the turban for a man and sometimes for a woman. On route to the crematorium the deceased is taken to the *gurdwara* [Sikh place of worship] where a *rumalla* [a square piece of silk] is placed on top of the shroud. At the crematorium, prayers . . . are said. The button is then pressed by a close male relative, usually the eldest son of the deceased. The next day, the ashes are collected and then—taken to a designated area of running water and immersed. . . . In India, for reasons of personal hygiene, the mourners bathe after the body has been cremated on the funeral pyre.

Beginning on the day of the death, adult relatives—or if they are unable to do so *granthis* from the gurdwara (people who perform readings)—usually take part in a complete reading of the Guru Granth Sahib (the Sikh holy book) at the home of the deceased or at the gurdwara. This reading is usually spaced over a period of ten days, and close family members, including children, would usually be expected to be present throughout. At the completion of the reading, a passage from the Guru Granth Sahib about belief and practices regarding death is read, followed by *kirtan* (songs in praise of God); the prayer *Ardas* is then said, followed by the sharing of *karah parshad* (specially blessed sweet pudding) and the eating of *langar* (a communal meal). If the deceased was the head of the family, the oldest son is given a turban to symbolise the taking on of responsibility for the family. . . .

Islamic Burial Customs

The Islamic concept of death is quite simple, the idea being that "from God (Allah) we have emerged and to God we return." Consequently, the official mourning period tends to be relatively short, usually not more than three days. Widows mourn for a year in the Middle East and North Africa. The next of kin mourn for forty days, however this does not include the deceased's spouse or children.

When death is imminent, the person is asked to declare their faith by repeating the simple formula: "God is One and Muhammad is His Prophet."

The Imam (the prayer leader at the mosque) is informed as soon as possible after death and prayers from the Qur'an (Koran) are recited over the body.

According to Islamic religious traditions, the prescribed mode of disposal of the body is burial.

The body is then taken to the Funeral Director's premises where it is washed by family members of the same gender as the deceased. This ritual is usually performed in a room that has been purified and from which all statues and religious symbols have been removed; special arrangements can be made with the Funeral Director to ensure that these beliefs, fundamental to the Islamic faith, are respected. After the body has been washed, it is swathed in a simple white cotton sheet or shroud; all Muslims are dressed alike to symbolize their equality before God. The body is then placed in an unlined coffin.

According to Islamic religious traditions, the prescribed mode of disposal of the body is burial. The burial of the body should take place before noon. If a person dies in the afternoon or during the night, they are buried the next morning before noon. If they die midday or thereabouts, then they are most likely to be buried the next morning, as burying after sunset is not customary. However, delays are inevitable, as there are various legal formalities that have to be completed before a certificate for disposal is given by the Registrar of Births and Deaths. Nevertheless, custom prescribes that the burial should take place with the minimum delay.

The usual practice is for the deceased to be taken to the mosque, where special prayers are recited, before proceeding to the graveyard. A brief prayer session is also held at the cemetery. The body is then buried in the grave with the head and right-hand side facing Makkah [Islamic holy city in Saudi Arabia]. . . .

Jewish Funeral Traditions

Jews believe in one God who created the universe. The Jewish Sabbath begins at sunset on Friday and ends an hour after sunset on Saturday, and commemorates the seventh day when God rested after the Creation. During this time religious Jews do not travel, write, cook or use electrical equipment.

Unless death occurs after sunset on Friday, in which case the burial is postponed until Sunday, the Orthodox Jewish tradition prescribes that funerals should take place within twenty-four hours. No professional undertakers are involved since all arrangements are made through the Synagogue. The body is dressed in a white shroud (*kittel*), which is then placed in a plain wooden coffin. Men are buried with a prayer shawl (*tallith*) with its tassels cut off.

While the body is in the house, Jews believe that it should not be left unattended. Candles are placed at the head and the foot of the coffin and sons or other near relatives of the deceased maintain a constant vigil. If no relatives are present, professional mourners are called in.

The rabbi is sent for as soon as death occurs. He or she returns to the house of mourning an hour or so before the funeral is due to start to offer special prayers for the deceased. Close relatives of the dead person usually gather at the house of mourning, dressed in old clothes from which a piece is ritually cut as a mark of grief. Traditionally this torn garment is worn throughout the seven days of intensive mourning (*shiveh*).

According to the orthodox [Jewish] tradition, cremation is forbidden.

After prayers offered by the rabbi at the house, the coffin is carried out and mourners usually follow on foot to the cemetery. If the cemetery is not within walking distance, transport is permitted, but many Orthodox Jews insist on covering at least part of the way on foot.

Progressive liberal Jews permit cremation. However according to the orthodox tradition, cremation is forbidden, as human beings are created in the image of God and it would therefore be wrong to deliberately destroy a body.

At the cemetery the dead body is taken to a special room. Mourners usually wait outside until the coffin is placed in the centre of the room. Then the men stand on the left and the women stand on the right of the coffin. There are no flowers or music at the funeral ceremony, ensuring that there is no distinction made between rich and poor. Prayers and psalms are recited and the rabbi makes a special mention of the virtues of the person who has died.

The coffin is then carried to the grave followed by the mourners. The sons and brothers of the deceased shovel some earth on the coffin. After the burial the special prayer for the dead, the *Kaddish*, is recited for the first time by the male relatives. A special meal is provided of eggs, salt-herrings and bagels. Peas or lentils are also suitable foods to serve on this occasion as, according to Jewish tradition, roundness signifies life. . . .

Buddhist Beliefs

Buddhists believe that they live a succession of lives; *samsara* is the word used to describe the endless cycle of birth, death and rebirth in various states (e.g. human, divine, animal, etc.) and in many different planes (e.g. happy, unhappy). Life in *samsara* continues until the believer attains an enlightened state of permanent, lasting happiness called *nirvana*: the ultimate goal of all Buddhist practice. Death is seen as a prelude to existence in another state. According to Buddha's teaching, no state lasts forever. The plane of rebirth is determined by a person's *kamma*, which is the sum total of wholesome and unwholesome actions performed in previous existences. In order to reach enlightenment, the Buddha's teachings, called the Noble Eightfold Path, should be followed. Until this state is reached we continue circling on in *samsara*.

One, two or three days after death the body is either buried or cremated.

Buddhists place great importance on the state of mind at the moment of death. When death is imminent a monk is called to chant from religious texts, or relatives may introduce some religious objects to generate wholesome thoughts into the person's mind, because the last thought before death will condition the first thought of the next life.

One, two or three days after death, the body is either buried or cremated. At the funeral a monk leads the congregation in the traditional Buddhist manner, offering respect to the Buddha, the *Dhamma* (his teaching), and the *Sangha* (the community of enlightened beings). Following this, the congregation accepts the *Five Precepts*, which are guidelines for—and commitment to—the leading of a moral life.

If a cremation takes place, it is traditional for a nephew of the deceased to press the button that draws the curtain on the coffin and consigns it to the furnace. Sometimes the ashes are kept in an urn, which may be stored in a monument built specifically for this purpose; alternatively they may be scattered. . . .

Christian Practices

Christians believe in one God who has revealed himself as Father, Son and Holy Spirit. This is described as the Holy Trinity. Central to Christian belief is Jesus of Nazareth in whom God assumed human form. The sacred text for Christians is the New Testament, which contains a code for living based on the life and teaching of Jesus. The resurrection of Jesus— when he returned to life after being crucified—is integral to the belief in Jesus' claim and offer of a life after death in heaven. Depending on the aspect of the central mysteries stressed by a particular Christian tradition, death can produce feelings of fear, resignation or hope.

After death the body of the dead person may be moved to the undertaker's Chapel of Rest. The word "chapel" does not necessarily indicate a place of worship, though in the case of believers the Funeral Director often arranges candles round the coffin and displays a cross in the room.

Instead of burial, some Christians may choose cremation.

Some Roman Catholics or High Church Anglicans transfer the corpse to their church on the evening before the funeral; following the ritual reception of the body into the church, it remains there overnight. In some [places], however, the coffin is brought to the house the evening before the funeral and transported from there to the church. The next morning a funeral service or requiem mass is celebrated during which the priest or minister wear black vestments.

The final ritual in Christian burial is the graveside committal where the minister leads the mourners in prayer as the body is lowered into the grave.

Instead of burial, some Christians may choose cremation. The ashes of the deceased may be scattered in a Garden of Remembrance or elsewhere. Alternatively, they may be placed in an urn and interred in a cemetery. Some families keep the ashes at home. If the ashes are to be scattered in the Garden of Remembrance, the family may choose the garden and the precise place of dispersal, and if they wish, they may return a few days later to witness the scattering of the ashes. . . .

Humanist Practice

Humanists believe that we only have one life and that we should make the best of it. We should try to live happy and fulfilled lives and help others to do so and the best way to achieve this is by living responsibly, thinking rationally about right and wrong, considering the consequences of our actions and trying to do the right thing. Humanists are concerned to make the world a better place in which to live, not only for people alive today, but also for future generations—especially as the lives of their descendants represent the only sort of immortality in which humanists believe.

[Humanists] do not believe in any kind of life after death, but believe that we live on in other people's memories of us.

Humanists ask themselves the same questions as everyone else: Why am I here? What's the purpose of life? How did life begin? What will happen to me when I die? They look for evidence before they take on a belief, and so are more likely to believe the results of scientific research or what their own experiences tell them—or remain open-minded about questions—rather than to believe what someone else says. Humanists tend to think about these big questions for themselves. Some questions may not have answers, or we might not like the most probable answers.

Humanists experience the same feeling of loss and sadness at the death of a loved one as anyone else does. But they accept death as the natural and inevitable end to life. They do not believe in any kind of life after death, but believe that we live on in other people's memories of us, in the work we have done while we are alive, and in our children.

There are no specific or obligatory rituals to be followed either by the bereaved or by those who wish to express their condolences. An expression of sympathy, an acknowledgement of the bereaved person's feeling of grief and the offer of a listening ear are more likely to be appreciated than any suggestion that the deceased has gone "to a better place" (which may contradict what the family believe).

Humanists may choose to be cremated or buried and the ceremony can take place anywhere, though it is most commonly held at a crematorium where, if possible, any religious symbols will be removed or covered up.

At a humanist funeral there will be no suggestion that the deceased has gone on to another life: the ceremony is intended to celebrate the life that was lived. The humanist funeral officiate will have spent time with the bereaved relatives and together they will have planned a ceremony that properly honours the person's life and, hopefully, brings some comfort to everyone who attends as they are reminded of how their lives have been enriched through knowing the deceased. At the funeral the officiate will talk about the person's life and what they achieved and it is usual for family members or friends to read personal tributes. The ceremony may also involve suitable readings, poetry or music, and there may be a brief period of silence to allow people attending the ceremony time for their own private reflection or—if they have religious beliefs—for prayer.

2

The Dead Should Be Buried

Michael Cahill

Michael Cahill is the past chair of the Chicago Archdiocesan Pastoral Council, and an adjunct faculty member at Mundelein Seminary.

The Catholic Church traditionally has taught both that the human soul is immortal, and that the body will be physically resurrected when Christ returns. Cremation, in that it destroys the body, indicates a lack of faith in the physical resurrection of the body. For this reason, cremation was forbidden to Catholics until 1963, and is still discouraged. In addition, because the body is sacred, it should be preserved, be present at the funeral for mourners to see, and be buried with respect, rather than whisked away to a crematorium to be destroyed.

I took my usual deep breath before heading into the funeral home. I both dread and look forward to wakes and funerals. I dread them because they so vividly remind me of my own mortality. I look forward to them because I get to see the "guest of honor" one more time, say goodbye, pay my respects, and pray for their resurrection.

When I walked into the parlor, I immediately saw the kneeler and headed toward it to pray. Suddenly I stopped. Something felt awkward and strange. Then I realized what was wrong. There was no body. I stood frozen, not sure what to do. A friend approached and said, "There she is." But I still didn't see her.

Michael Cahill, "Don't Bury Death: A Catholic Argument Against Cremation," *U.S. Catholic*, December 2006. Reproduced by permission.

My friend walked me closer to the kneeler, then I saw the urn. The family had decided on cremation and had cremated her before the services. I turned toward the kneeler again but then moved on, unable to kneel. I couldn't pray before the urn because it wasn't truly her, any more than Chicago's Wrigley Field would be the city's baseball shrine if it had burned to the ground.

Standing at the back of the parlor, I felt guilty and old-fashioned all at once. It wasn't that I was consciously refusing to kneel or trying to make a statement. Yet I knew what I had failed to do was at best politically incorrect. But still I couldn't kneel.

Cremation and the Resurrection of the Body

For many centuries the church has taught the doctrine of the immortality of the soul and the resurrection of the body. Until 1963 it also condemned cremation because it was thought such an act indicated a lack of belief in resurrection. Although the church now allows cremation, the Catholic Order of Christian Funerals (OCF) reminds Catholics that cremation "does not enjoy the same value as burial of the body."

Even when the family chooses cremation, the church recommends that the body be cremated after the funeral Mass since "the presence of the human body better expresses the values which the church affirms in the [funeral] rites."

While it is true that cremation is part of a religious ritual in other religions, it is decidedly not Catholic tradition, especially not in 21st-century American Catholicism.

What are those values? "The church's belief in the sacredness of the human body and the resurrection of the dead has traditionally found expression in the care taken to prepare the bodies of the deceased for burial," according to the OCF.

Burial Is Preferable to Cremation

Does this mean that I am making the case that burial is preferable to cremation, and that in the case of cremation, it must take place after the funeral? Absolutely. The heart of that case lies in two phrases quoted above. The first phrase, "the care taken to prepare the bodies," has to do with us, the living; while the second, "the sacredness of the human body and the resurrection of the dead," has to do with the dead.

While it is true that cremation is part of a religious ritual in other religions, it is decidedly not Catholic tradition, especially not in 21st-century American Catholicism. There may be understandable and good reasons to choose cremation, including cost, the environmental impact of burial, and the wishes of the deceased. In the U.S. church, however, cremation most often serves as a way to move through a death quickly with as little bother and fuss as possible.

We are a society with no time for death or for the slow and sacred rituals that accompany both the dead and us to our loved one's final resting place. We have long been removed from the personal care of the dead body, with the body prepared out of sight at the mortuary. Even more, cremation, usually performed in private with few if any family present, leaves little or no physical reminder of death at all.

What better sign of our belief in the resurrection of the body than our preparation, physical and spiritual, of that body to meet the Lord.

One Chicago parish has responded by having a bereavement ministry through which parishioners actually come to the house of the deceased and help the family bathe the body one final time and prepare it for burial.

Perhaps most of us are unlikely to become engaged in the physical preparation of the body, but at least we should ensure such care is taken. We should witness it and continue that care through the rituals, formal and informal, that make up the wake and funeral. We are, after all, a sacramental church, and what better sign of our belief in the resurrection of the body than our preparation, physical and spiritual, of that body to meet the Lord.

When I was young, I was taught that my body was the temple of the Holy Spirit. There are a lot of messages about the importance of our bodies embedded in the culture today, but few, if any, honor the body's sacredness. Many, in fact, objectify our bodies so as to make them devoid of personhood. No wonder it is more difficult to persuade people to bring the body of the deceased to church. After all, what difference does it make? Can't God raise a cremated body as easily as one that was buried? That's true, of course, since resurrection is more than mere resuscitation.

But the preservation of a loved one's body has more to do with us than it does with God. Our loved one's body is a sacramental sign of our belief in the resurrection. As the OCF puts it, "This is the body once washed in Baptism, anointed with the oil of salvation, and fed with the bread of life. This is the body whose hands clothed the poor and embraced the sorrowing. Indeed, the human body is so inextricably associated with the human person that it is hard to think of a human person apart from his or her body."

The woman whose wake I attended, for example, I had known for almost 20 years. She was a physically large woman, and her loud laughter could fill a room. Her later years were plagued by much depression, and her large physique ironically made that depression stand out. At times it made her look small. It was that embodied spirit, the sacramental sign of her body, that I missed at her wake, a sign that spoke of both her joy and her pain.

In a recent issue of the archdiocesan newspaper of Chicago, Cardinal Francis George [the archbishop of Chicago] recounted a story that St. Teresa of Avila [a sixteenth-century

Spanish holy woman] told about the devil appearing to her disguised as the risen Christ. Teresa immediately understood there was an imposter in her midst and told the devil she knew he was not Christ "because you have no wounds." The cardinal went on to remind his readers that "the resurrection of the body is harder to imagine than the immortality of the soul but both are truths of faith," and that "too seldom do we think of risen bodies, glorious and eternal. We will bear our wounds for eternity, but we will do so joyfully and with complete freedom."

Saying Goodbye to the Body

Last summer I attended another wake and funeral, this time for my mother. What a contrast it was to my friend's. My mother died from Alzheimer's disease, and one of my sisters insisted that she was laid out with a scowl that accurately described her attitude about having suffered from Alzheimer's. As I looked at Mom that evening, I wondered how someone so small had borne seven children. I marveled even more that someone whose mind and body had both shriveled in recent years had once been so formidable a woman. I delighted in the memory of her beautiful singing voice, which could immediately hush a room.

My sister Meg insisted on seeing the casket being closed for the final time. I stayed in the parlor with her while the room cleared out. In the last months of her life, my mother's right leg became permanently locked in the shape of an upside down V. We simply couldn't straighten her leg. So when the funeral directors had to open the bottom half of the casket lid in order to close the whole casket once and for all, there was that right leg sticking up. My sister Meg turned to me with a sad smile and said, "It was good to see that leg one more time."

Meg lived right across the street from Mom. She lived with that leg, that body, every day for many long years as the disease ravaged Mom's mind and body. She had, in a sense, taken great care "to prepare the body of the deceased for the funeral." Now, with grace and humor, she got her chance to say goodbye to that sacred body, that temple of the Holy Spirit, one last time just before we left to celebrate Christ's Resurrection, and with it, the resurrection of the body.

3

Burying the Dead Pollutes Groundwater

Richard D.L. Fulton

Richard D.L. Fulton is news editor of the Emmitsburg Dispatch *in Emmitsburg, Maryland.*

Old cemeteries have the potential of contaminating groundwater with a host of dangerous chemicals used in embalming, including formaldehyde and arsenic. Both wooden and metal caskets decompose over time, and the embalming chemicals can then leach into the groundwater. Because the government does not require cemeteries to have landfill-type liners and does not do adequate testing of groundwater near cemeteries, it is likely that cemeteries pose a serious threat to drinking water. Citizens should insist that local government establish safety standards to protect groundwater from cemetery pollution.

A New Jersey woman reported in 1990 that she believed her drinking water was making her ill. N.J. environmental authorities ran tests on the water, which came from an on-site well, and found no contaminants.

Still, she insisted the water was causing her sickness. An expensive, full-spectrum test revealed that the water was laced with formaldehyde, a chemical used to embalm corpses.

Although the investigating agency remained at a loss to explain the odd contaminant, the discovery during the investigation of a nearby cemetery raised a red flag.

A Potentially Grave Situation

No direct connection was ever made between the cemetery and the presence of formaldehyde in the immediate drinking water in the above incident.

As one employee of the investigating agency stated, "Not everyone was agreed that formaldehyde was coming from the cemetery," noting that the nearby cemetery had been created for veterans, and dated back to a period when arsenic was the primary embalming chemical.

Cemeteries can be laced with a myriad of chemicals . . . that could easily transfer from age-old decomposing bodies into groundwater.

The incident passed by without significant media fanfare, probably because the press itself never foresaw the potential ramifications of cemetery contamination, since no direct link had been made during the 1990 investigation.

But, in truth, cemeteries can be laced with a myriad of chemicals and have never been significantly regulated to control or monitor contaminants that could easily transfer from the age-old decomposing bodies into the groundwater.

The U.S. Environmental Protection Agency has established action levels for every potential contaminant a cemetery could generate. But historically, those regulations have only been applied to industry, landfills, wastewater facility discharges and farm runoff, not to cemeteries.

Oddly, cemeteries seem to have been neglected, even though the Environmental Engineering and Marine Geoscience Division of the Council for Geoscience indicated as early as 1997, "Research shows that poorly sited cemeteries pose a threat of groundwater pollution, at least equal in magnitude to that posed by conventional waste-disposal sites."

Formaldehyde and Groundwater

The most prevalent embalming fluid used since the early 1900s has been formalin, commonly comprised of water containing 37 percent formaldehyde with 10 to 15 percent methyl alcohol added to reduce polymerization. EPA has classified formaldehyde as a probable human carcinogen.

According to the Agency for Toxic Substance and Disease Registry, "High levels of exposure (to formaldehyde) may cause some type of cancers. . . . Ingestion of as little as one ounce of a solution containing 37 percent formaldehyde has been reported to cause death in an adult."

Formaldehyde is not a good thing to have in the drinking water, but the good news is it does not last long once discharged to the environment, because it is actually a gas and evaporates once exposed to the air. The bad news is, as the 1990s incident suggests, it might not always evaporate while traveling through underground water conveyance systems, natural and manmade.

Bodies were once buried in wooden caskets, which were phased out in favor of metal ones. While one would think that metal caskets would prevent embalming fluid from escaping, according to John L. Konefes and Michael K. McGee, as stated in the paper, "Old Cemeteries, Arsenic, and Health Safety". . . "Both wooden and metal caskets will eventually degrade and begin to allow contact of the embalmed remains with the environment."

Probably one of the deadliest pollutants associated with burials in relative recent history is arsenic, an extremely poisonous chemical.

Thus, while formaldehyde does disperse into the environment faster than older types of embalming fluids, if it does not have a chance to evaporate, it may still wind up in drinking water. But no one routinely tests for formaldehyde unless some indicator suggests its presence.

Arsenic as an Embalming Fluid

Probably one of the deadliest pollutants associated with burials in relatively recent history is arsenic, an extremely poisonous chemical. While no longer used in embalming, great quantities of it were used a little over a century ago.

"From 1856 to 1873, six patents were issued for (embalming) fluids that contained arsenic, from as little as four ounces to as much as 12 pounds of arsenic per body," according to Konefes and McGee. Arsenic continued to be used into the early 1900s when it was banned and replaced with formalin.

It was most widely used when bodies were buried in wooden caskets, and arsenic persists in the environment, meaning it does not evaporate or readily break down into other less harmful ingredients.

Researchers . . . have acknowledged that deadly chemicals associated with the embalming process pose potential threats to drinking water supplies.

It has been suggested that, at least the arsenic used in the past, has long since been washed from the soils and dispersed. Konefes and McGee note, however, that recent tests of a Civil War grave revealed the continued presence of arsenic. "This is firm documentation that arsenic embalmed remains can carry the arsenic residue for many years," they wrote.

The EPA mandates that local water authorities test for arsenic, but private well owners are on their own. According to the Agency for Toxic Substances and Disease Registry, ingesting high levels of arsenic can be fatal. Studies have also shown that ingesting inorganic arsenic "can increase the risk of skin cancer and cancer in the lungs, bladder, liver, kidney and prostate."

Less used in embalming, but still potentially dangerous, were mercury and creosote, according to Konefes and McGee.

In addition to actual embalming materials, normal graveyard maintenance can involve pesticides, herbicides and discharges of equipment fuel or oil. In addition, ongoing debate continues about the extent of the danger from actual biological agents such as viruses and bacteria, released from decomposed bodies.

Endangered Water Supplies

Researchers in Canada, the United Kingdom and South Africa have published papers on cemetery contamination and have acknowledged that deadly chemicals associated with the embalming process pose potential threats to drinking water supplies.

But the United States has shown little interest. . . . Both EPA and Maryland Department of the Environment representatives acknowledged that no regulations require cemetery owners to monitor the discharges to the environment from their burial sites.

No government agency mandates that future cemeteries be lined as per solid waste and hazardous waste landfills and no one seems to be accountable for any action. But this lack of regulation is somewhat universal.

Macclesfield Borough Council, England, posted the following on their Web site "Our ignorance of the consequences of using this chemical (formaldehyde embalming fluids) is a cause for concern. In particular, the chemical is used by funeral directors and embalmers who carry no responsibility for its impact on the cemetery, crematorium or community."

The Need for Action

Aside from the families considering burial alternatives, some government measures could be implemented to protect drinking water in the immediate and long-term future, including: expanding water-testing criteria for water supplies which draw from groundwater or reservoirs near cemeteries, establishing monitoring wells up and down gradient from cemeteries, installing landfill-type liners beneath proposed cemeteries, and, in worst-case scenarios, site remediation.

The best first step is to involve local government, since it is at that level that some initial action could be considered and possibly implemented, including establishing standards for present and future cemeteries.

4

Burials Can Be Environmentally Friendly

Kirsten Scharnberg

Kirsten Scharnberg is a national correspondent for the Chicago Tribune.

A growing trend for the disposal of human bodies is what is known as "green burial." People are buried without embalment, in biodegradable coffins in a location such as Ramsey Creek Preserve in South Carolina, the first conservation burial grounds. Because bodies quickly decompose and nurture vegetation, green burial helps the environment rather than harming it. In addition, green burial grounds contribute to land conservation. In many such places, the land has been placed in a conservation trust to ensure it will remain a natural setting.

When Billy Campbell's father died a number of years ago, the family did what was expected at the time: Bury him in a historic cemetery behind the family's Methodist church.

The setting was lovely and bucolic, but Campbell, a devoted land conservationist, couldn't stop thinking, "With what we spent on that funeral, I could have bought 5 or 10 acres and created a more permanent memorial to him."

The First Conservation Burial Ground

With his father's death in mind, Campbell in 1998 decided to try to marry the multibillion-dollar U.S. funeral industry with the nation's growing land conservation and environmental

Kirsten Scharnberg, "For Growing Ranks in U.S., Preference to Go Out Green," *Chicago Tribune*, November 26, 2007. Reproduced by permission.

movements. On 38 acres in western South Carolina, he opened the first conservation burial ground in the United States, a stunningly beautiful stretch of woods, grassland and lush creek beds where people are buried with the simplicity of centuries past and where the proceeds go toward preserving and restoring the land.

Known as "green burial," the concept, which is gaining popularity nationwide, essentially follows the religious pronouncement of "ashes to ashes, dust to dust."

People are buried without embalming chemicals, their remains refrigerated or kept on dry ice to prevent decay before family viewings. Bodies are placed into the ground in simple pine or cardboard caskets that will quickly decompose, and some people choose to be buried in nothing more than a white cotton shroud or a beloved family quilt.

There are no vaults. Grave markers consist of small, flat stones natural to the area. And the money spent on the plot— about $2,000 at the South Carolina cemetery—helps fund a land trust that will forever keep the area pristine as well as replant native trees and vegetation around the grave site.

[Environmentalists] charge that enough metal goes into the production of caskets . . . each year to rebuild the Golden Gate Bridge.

"Through this kind of burial, people have a real opportunity to be part of the healing of the land," said Campbell's wife, Kimberley, who oversees much of the day-to-day operation of Ramsey Creek Preserve, the burial grounds the couple started in Westminster, S.C. "In the U.S., so often we think of nature as a place of recreation. But this concept is a way to connect people to the land through tradition and ritual, and there are few traditions and rituals more important to us as those that surround death."

The Popularity of Green Burials Grows Quickly

Indeed, "green" cemeteries have taken off quickly in the decade since Campbell's cemetery opened. In recent years, similar ones have opened in California, Florida, Texas, New York, Washington and Maine. Three more are in the works, in Maine, New Mexico and Georgia. And in response to growing demand, many traditional cemeteries throughout the country are considering devoting portions of their land to burials where remains are not embalmed and vaults are not used.

John Bucci, a Wisconsin funeral director who serves southern Wisconsin and northern Illinois, said he is beginning to see the green burial trend creep into the Midwest. A prominent Milwaukee cemetery recently converted a significant portion of its acreage to a green cemetery and has returned the land to its original wooded condition. Bucci has yet to find a cemetery in Illinois that has gone so far but says he hopes that some will begin to respond to the growing demand.

"What happened 30 years ago with the rise in cremation could eventually happen with green burials," said Joe Sehee, executive director of the Green Burial Council. "People like the idea of their burial being part of a national conservation strategy. . . . They want their last act to be meaningful, something that heals the land and the soul and connects them to something bigger and longer-lasting than a coffin or an insurance policy."

Funeral Directors Find Fault

But green burials also have downsides, mainstream funeral directors contend. They say that makeup application, often used to make the deceased look better after long illnesses, is difficult without embalming. They worry that doing viewings quickly—usually within 24 to 48 hours to beat any decomposition—is sometimes too fast for grieving families. They say that digging graves in some parts of the country can be next to impossible for weeks on end in winter, but that unembalmed bodies should not be kept unburied for that long. And they assert that embalming cuts down on the risk, however small, of disease transmission from buried corpses.

"Embalming is the technical side of what we do," said funeral director Bucci. "For many of us it's been very hard to hear from the green movement that they believe there is not only no value but actual harm in what we do."

A Green Burial Response

Proponents of green burial counter all that. They say most cultures view their dead quickly and without trauma with no embalming. They say the simple burials often are healing for families because they can dig the graves by hand, build the caskets with locally found wood and lower the body into the ground themselves.

[Green burial advocates] urge embracing the decomposition of the body and what it gives back to the environment rather than fighting the inevitable.

Greensprings, a green cemetery in upstate New York, has a ground warmer that can be used to soften frozen earth for digging in the winter. And advocates say that only in the rarest of circumstances would disease transmission be a concern.

"A lot of the public is completely confused about what is or isn't allowed when it comes to burial," said Mark Harris, the author of *Grave Matters: A Journey Through the Modern Funeral Industry to a Natural Way of Burial.* "They believe embalming is required, when in fact that is almost never the case in any state in the nation. Look at Jewish burials, for example: They do not embalm, and that's absolutely legal everywhere."

Environmentalists have long been critical of the funeral industry in the U.S. Cemeteries often are on ground cleared of trees for a new forest of marble headstones. Critics, including

Harris and the Green Burial Council, say that nearly a million gallons of toxic embalming fluid is buried in cemetery ground every year, a potential risk to groundwater supplies. They further charge that enough metal goes into the production of caskets and burial vaults each year to rebuild the Golden Gate Bridge and that enough concrete is used on vaults to build a two-lane road from New York to Detroit.

Returning to Old Burial Customs

So proponents of green burials advocate burying the nation's dead the way people were buried for centuries, until the 1900s when embalming became popular in the U.S. and Canada. (In virtually no other part of the world is embalming with formaldehyde used as frequently as it is in North America.) They urge embracing the decomposition of the body and what it gives back to the environment rather than fighting the inevitable.

"There is no chemical or coffin or vault that we can use that will forever stop a body from decomposing or from being affected by the elements," said the Green Burial Council's Sehee, a former Jesuit lay minister.

People nationwide are choosing green burials, even if such cemeteries do not exist in their home states; at Ramsey Creek, for example, people from California to New Jersey have had their bodies shipped on dry ice to be buried there.

Harris believes the trend toward green burials is typical of Baby Boomers.

It is not just those with environmental urges who are choosing green burials. Many simply want their final place of rest to be beautiful, natural and uncomplicated.

"As Baby Boomers approach the end of their lives, they are going to bring a very do-it-yourself mentality to death," Harris said. "Green burials isn't just about preserving the environment, though that's a big part of it for a lot of people. It's also significantly cheaper. The burials tend to be simple affairs that are led and controlled by the families themselves. And it is a return to tradition that speaks to old-fashioned American values of thrift and self-sufficiency, and that appeals to a large swath of America, not just environmentalists."

Conserving the Land

For those who advocate green burial, it has been a no-brainer to link the burials with land conservation. Consider the model of the Galisteo River Basin preserve south of Santa Fe, a 13,000-acre former ranch covered with bonsai, pinion and juniper trees. Plans for Galisteo call for part of the acreage to become a sprawling green cemetery while other portions become orchards, meadows and sites for a non-denominational chapel and an environmental education center. Every person who donates $4,000 to the conservancy that oversees the project receives the right to be buried there.

Yet it is not just those with environmental urges who are choosing green burials. Many simply want their final place of rest to be beautiful, natural and uncomplicated.

Billy Campbell recently saw exactly that when a man from Westminster chose to buy a plot at Ramsey Creek. When Campbell told the man, known for a curmudgeonly streak, that he was surprised by his burial choice, the man said, "Listen, I love the woods. It's you . . . environmentalists that I can't stand."

The man paid $4,000 for plots for him and his wife. He got eternity in the woods. Campbell got money to preserve the trees and land.

"With green burial, maybe everyone wins in the end," Kimberley Campbell said with a laugh.

Green Burials Can Be Less Costly

Green burials often are significantly less expensive than traditional burials.

The National Funeral Directors Association estimates the average cost of a funeral to be about $6,500, a number that often is much higher after the costs of a burial plot, headstone and cemetery burial fees are included.

In contrast, burial at Ramsey Creek Preserve, a green cemetery in South Carolina, can be as low as about $3,600, including the price of the plot, burial fees and the $1,200 cost of working with a local funeral home for transport and refrigeration of the body before burial.

At Greensprings, a green cemetery in upstate New York, the cost of plot and burial fees comes in at just under $1,000.

But in areas of the country where land is more expensive, green isn't always the cheapest option. At Forever Fernwood, a green cemetery in Mill Valley, Calif., plots alone can cost up to $9,000.

5

Cremation Harms
the Environment

DeeDee Correll

DeeDee Correll is a Los Angeles Times *staff writer.*

When the dead are cremated, their dental fillings release mercury into the air. Mercury is a very dangerous substance for human health and causes serious damage to the nervous system. Members of the funeral industry argue that the amount of mercury emitted from crematoria is not harmful. However, cremation is growing in popularity and more people die with fillings now than in the past. Consequently, mercury emissions will rise and damage the environment unless cremationists install filters to their smokestacks, or remove the teeth of the dead before cremation.

R ick Allnutt has closed all but one section of his funeral home on the north end of town.

The chapel is dark and quiet, the reception hall bare. But in the bay out back, two side-by-side ovens rumble as the 1,650-degree heat blasts two corpses into bone and ash.

Allnutt has moved the rest of the business to another location and wants to move his crematory to a site near a cemetery in Larimer County [Colorado], but he has reached a stalemate with health officials there. They are concerned about what they see as a potential health risk to the living—mercury being released into the atmosphere from dental fillings of the cremated.

They want him to do something that may be unprecedented in this country: Install a filter on his crematory's smokestack or extract teeth of the deceased before cremation.

Allnutt refuses to do either, calling the first option too expensive and the second ghoulish.

"I'm not going to be the only one in the world who says I'll pull teeth from dead bodies," he said.

Across the United States, the issue is cropping up: Do mercury emissions from dental fillings of corpses incinerated in crematories pose a threat? And if so, how should it be handled?

In Colorado, it's something that health officials are only now examining, said Mark McMillan, manager of the Department of Public Health and Environment's mercury program.

"We're on the cusp of starting to understand it," he said.

The cremation industry, on the other hand, insists there's no evidence of danger and calls Allnutt's situation "a dangerous precedent."

In humans, mercury damages the nervous system and can harm childhood development.

At issue are amalgam dental fillings. Amalgam—an alloy of mercury with another metal such as silver, copper or tin—is commonly used to fill cavities.

When a body is burned, mercury from such fillings vaporizes. Once released into the atmosphere, mercury returns to Earth in rain or snow, ending up in lakes and other bodies of water where it can lead to elevated levels of mercury in fish. In humans, mercury damages the nervous system and can harm childhood development. Power plants, especially those that burn coal, are by far the largest source of preventable mercury releases; Environmental Protection Agency regulations have been adopted to reduce those emissions.

As cremation continues to gain popularity in the United States, the issue may gain more traction.

According to the Cremation Assn. of North America, a 2005 survey found 46% of Americans planned to choose cremation, compared with 31% in 1990. Its use varies widely by region: In Nevada and Hawaii, two-thirds of bodies were cremated in 2005; in a number of Southern states, a tenth were.

The EPA does not regulate emissions from crematories, spokeswoman Margot Perez-Sullivan said. It estimates that about 600 pounds of mercury, less than 1% of all mercury emissions, come from crematories in the U.S. every year. (By contrast, the British government requires new crematories to install filters to cut mercury emissions, according to the British Broadcasting Corp. It estimates that fillings account for 16% of mercury emissions in the United Kingdom, where the cremation rate is greater than 70%.)

In recent years, several states have taken stabs at the issue.

In Minnesota, state Sen. John Marty repeatedly has sought—and failed—to pass a law requiring crematory operators to remove teeth or install filters.

He said crematories in Minnesota emit an estimated 68 pounds of mercury every year—3% to 5% of mercury emissions in the state. Though coal-fired power plants constitute the greatest problem, Marty said, "we have to go after every source. But it's not easy politically because people are really squeamish about talking about corpses."

In 2005 Maine lawmakers considered, but defeated, a similar bill.

Colorado does not regulate crematories' mercury emissions, which state health officials estimate at about 110 pounds per year.

But the [Colorado] state health department last year began examining the issue. Funded by the EPA, the effort seeks to reduce the amount of mercury emitted through voluntary partnerships with crematory operators, said McMillan, the program's manager.

So far, collaboration appears unlikely to succeed.

"Their assumptions are all incorrect," said Mark Matthews, a director for the Cremation Assn. of North America. "There's a battle over something that doesn't exist. The data doesn't add up, and the science isn't there."

He said no studies had found higher concentrations of mercury near crematories, and he pointed out that the EPA does not regulate them.

Even if there were a problem, Matthews said, the proposed solution is "unworkable." For one, he said, families often have viewings before a cremation; removing the teeth probably would mean disfiguring the face. And the idea is upsetting to grieving relatives, he said. "To suggest that we ought to remove the teeth is completely insensitive to the families we serve."

In Larimer County, the issue came to a head this year when Allnutt applied for a special-use permit to relocate his crematory, which conducts 450 cremations per year.

Neighbors immediately seized on the mercury issue.

In a worst-case scenario, a model found that mercury levels could rise above the recommended short-term exposure levels.

"There's a very real problem," said Dennis Lynch, a retired forest sciences professor at Colorado State University who read the available research and wrote a paper on his findings. "Crematoriums have gotten a free pass for a long time. We should be asking them to do their civic responsibility and do prevention of some kind."

Allnutt, who owns a chain of funeral homes in northern Colorado, hired a consultant to estimate the facility's potential effects. In a worst-case scenario, a model found that mercury levels could rise above recommended short-term exposure limits.

The findings persuaded Doug Ryan, Larimer County's environmental-health planner, to recommend that county commissioners grant Allnutt's permit only if he agreed to reduce emissions. The county has the authority to do so, Ryan said, because applicants for special-use permits must show that their facility will be compatible with their surroundings. In this case, Ryan said, compatibility means preventing mercury exposure.

At a planning commission meeting in November, Allnutt made his stand, and the county planning commission, an advisory board, voted against granting him a permit. Allnutt hasn't decided whether to pursue a hearing before the Board of Commissioners.

The county was unfair, he said, in asking him to do something none of his competitors must do. Installing a smokestack filter at $500,000 would put him at an automatic disadvantage, he said.

But he also said he'll never pull teeth—even if it means getting out of the cremation business. "I won't do that," Allnutt said. "It's a moral issue."

Modern Crematories Are Environmentally Friendly

Paul F. Rahill

Paul F. Rahill is the president of Matthews International's Cremation Division and serves as the environmental consultant to the Cremation Association of North America.

Although people might disagree about what causes global warming, caring for the environment is everyone's concern, including the cremation industry. North American crematories meet all current environmental guidelines established by the U.S. Evironmental Protection Agency. In addition technologies work to both reduce emissions from crematory smokestacks, and also reduce the amount of fuel needed to cremate a body. Therefore, modern crematories can make cremation an even more environmentally friendly method of disposing of the dead.

Global warming has quickly become a household phrase as familiar to most of us as "Googling" and "IM." Feeling a step behind? Well, global warming is the very slow but steady increase in temperature of the earth's atmosphere. This gentle but growing increase in temperature has been linked by many experts to the melting of the polar ice caps, future extinction of animal species and the loss of viable farming for the poorest of the poor.

Getting the word out on this potential threat and delivering calls to action have been through quite an eclectic group

Paul F. Rahill, "'Greening' of Cremation in North America," Matthews Cremation Division, October 17, 2007. www.matthewscremation.com/industry/newsAndAnnouncements.asp.

that you would not normally expect: politicians and preachers, environmentalists and economists, celebrities and CEOs, scientists and school kids.

Taking Care of the Environment

True experts and scientists, however, line up on opposing sides of this issue filled with passion and armed with data, one side claiming global warming is man made while the other assures us it is a natural cycle of the earth as old as time itself. A skeptical friend of mine (now gray and wrinkled) smugly informed me that he participated in the first Earth Day event, over 25 years ago, where they were warning the masses of global cooling and the coming ice age!

Extensive testing by state, federal and independent agencies has shown time and time again that crematories operate well within the current environmental guidelines.

When you strip away the politics and posturing, what we are really talking about is taking care of the environment we will pass on to our children and grandchildren using the knowledge, skills and technology we have, all within reason. Care and concern for the environment may seem like the cause du jour but it really isn't. We can look as far back as the book of Genesis in which it says God placed man in the Garden of Eden to care for it and protect it.

North American Cremations Are Environmentally Friendly

So what does all this have to do with cremation? North American cremation practices have long been considered environmentally friendly as compared to many places around the world. Much of this has to do with North American crematories being located primarily in funeral homes and city centers where there was pressure from a strong need and desire to operate cremation equipment as smoke and odor free as possible. Our sincere desire to be good neighbors actually resulted in us being environmentally friendly at the same time, long before it was as wildly popular as it is today.

Extensive testing by state, federal and independent agencies has shown time and time again that crematories operate well within the current environmental guidelines. United States Environmental Protection Agency (USEPA) testing even resulted in human and animal cremation equipment being eliminated from the list of industries that were to be covered by new federal environmental regulations in 2005. . . .

Cleaner Emissions

Residence time is the amount of time the emissions from a cremation are held in the secondary chamber (after chamber) of the cremation equipment for the purposes of cleansing them. Many states require cremation equipment to be designed and operated to hold these gases [frac12] to 1 second which in most cases is more than adequate time. Most new "hot hearth" cremation equipment designs can now provide retention times of 2 seconds or greater, increasing the cleansing action of the cremation equipment which results in lower emissions from the cremation process. Longer retention times are also helpful when cremating large bodies and when tasking the cremation equipment to handle more and more cremations in a single day. It is difficult to add retention time to older or obsolete cremation equipment. There comes a time however when replacing and upgrading is the best course of action we can take.

Proper Temperature Is Important

Temperature of the secondary chamber, both adequate and steady, is critical in the proper operation of cremation equipment. Not enough temperature and there will be unwanted emissions from the exhaust stack, too much temperature and these unwanted emissions increase even more. So what is the "just right" temperature for cremation? Extensive environmental testing conducted jointly by the USEPA and CANA, the Cremation Association of North America, proved to be invaluable in solving this debate amongst environmental professionals. . . . A USEPA report on crematory environmental operations shows clearly that 1400°F is the ideal temperature. Emissions from cremation equipment increased significantly when the secondary chamber temperature was increased from 1400°F to 1600°F and then increased again from 1600°F to 1800°F.

Many states and provinces have been slow to adopt the findings of this breakthrough research however and as an industry [cremationists] will continue to educate, inform and nudge our government leaders to do what is best for all: environment, public and cremation professionals.

Temperature control systems, while standard on most new cremation systems, can be added or adapted to older and existing cremation equipment for reasonable costs which will eventually pay for it in fuel savings.

Keeping an Eye on the Stack

Opacity controls are optical scanning devices positioned in the cremation equipment exhaust stack to watch what is going up the stack and out to atmosphere. These devices can be configured to take action when they see something we don't want to occur. If they detect visible smoke entering the stack they can sound an audible alarm, turn on a warning light and will even take corrective action adjusting the fuel and air automatically, usually correcting any smoke condition within seconds. While these systems are not exactly new to . . . [the cremation] industry, their inclusion into cremation equipment designs has been limited to mostly only the more environmentally advanced cremation systems. Opacity controls vary in their complexity, however, basic designs work well for cremation equipment and are relatively easy to adjust, maintain and calibrate. The State of Florida recently adopted the requirement of opacity controls on all new cremation equipment beginning early 2007. More good news is that these systems can be added to most all existing and older designs for reasonable costs to the crematory owners.

New Technology

Newer cremation technology is also beginning to emerge or is at least currently emerging in more affordable designs. This technology can decrease the use of fossil fuels in the combustion system and decrease emissions from the cremation process, both a bonus to our environment.

Intuitive Logic Control (ILC) is an automated control system that depends less on the knowledge and expertise of the crematory operator and more on the reality of what he is going to cremate at that moment. All of us in the industry know we experience significant variables in the types of cremation containers we receive. Not only do the materials differ widely but the weight can range from 7 pounds to 170 pounds. We receive human remains for cremation ranging from 60 pounds to 600 pounds and those same bodies have varying fat tissue percentages from 4% to 40%. All these variables and others impact the cremation process and the decisions operators are faced with.

> *A common goal [cremationists] can all embrace is to learn as much as we can regarding our industry and the environment.*

Intuitive Logic Control systems only require the operator to answer a few questions and the ILC system calculates the options and sets the parameters based on many automatic inputs and logic programs. This reduces the opportunity for operator error which in turn will reduce the emissions from the cremation equipment, another win-win for everyone involved. ILC systems can be added to most new and existing cremation systems for costs that are well within reason for most North American crematories.

Fuel Savings

Oxygen [O_2] control is another available technology while not new has certainly improved in performance and price. Oxygen control systems measure O_2 levels in the exhaust gases at the exit of the secondary chamber of the cremation equipment. Controlling O_2 to optimum levels provides benefits on many levels. First, steady oxygen levels in the combustion process reduce emissions from the cremation equipment by more effectively cleansing them with ideal mixtures of O_2 along with the gases given off in the cremation process. Second, by controlling O_2 more closely to the level required, less fuel is needed to heat up any excess O_2 in the system. Reducing fuel consumption not only reduces money spent, it also reduces emissions by not burning the fuel which by itself creates unwanted emissions. Thirdly, tighter control of oxygen will impact the time required for cremation, reducing it along with the emissions and fuel consumption. Oxygen control systems are still considered pricey by some crematories but advances in technology and manufacturing have brought it into the realm of possibility for many new and existing crematories.

Beliefs and motivations surrounding global warming and the environment will vary amongst those in [the cremation] industry as will the ability to afford and install the newest and most effective green technology. However, a common goal ... [cremationists] can all embrace is to learn as much as we can regarding our industry and the environment, steadily moving toward improving our environmental signature in the communities we serve.

7

Contemporary Funerals Honor the Dead

Robert Kastenbaum

Robert Kastenbaum is the author of several books on death and dying. He is a professor emeritus in the School of Human Communication at Arizona State University.

Many people wonder if funerals are necessary in today's secular, high-tech world. One reason to continue funerals is that they connect people with human history. Another, more important, reason is that funerals allow living people to feel that they have helped send the dead on to whatever awaits them. Finally, funeral rituals provide a means through which survivors can honor their recently departed friend or family member. Contemporary technology and new ideas about funerals can help nonreligious people honor the dead in services of their own design.

W e can learn about a society from the questions asked as well as the answers provided. "Funerals are for the living" is a preemptory answer that often presents itself even before a question can be raised. This fast-trigger answer to an unasked question protects us from uncomfortable reflections about our beliefs and assumptions. Crawling through a convenient escape hatch, however, can be inconsistent with our responsibilities as human-service providers. We try to cultivate perspective, a readiness for reflection, and the nerve to cross into difficult territory when the situation so requires.

Robert Kastenbaum, "Why Funerals?" *Generations: Journal of the American Society on Aging*, vol. 28, no. 2, summer 2004, pp. 5–10. Copyright © 2004 American Society on Aging, San Francisco, California. www.asaging.org. Posted with permission.

Coming to the present case, we can be more helpful to people who are facing death-related issues if we are prepared to go beyond the formulaic answer to the question, Why funerals? Echoes from the past are resonating today within a high-tech society that has been trying hard not to listen. Beneath our whiz-bang, cybernetic, Palm-Pilot daily whirl we still have much in common with those who confronted death long before history found an enduring voice. Our orientation must somehow take into account both the distinctive characteristics of life in the early twenty-first century and our continuing bonds with all who have experienced the loss of loved ones. We begin, then, a retrospective view and then look at funerals in our own time. . . .

We would recognize the anguish of newly bereaved people thousands of years ago and they would recognize ours.

The Dead: Vulnerable and Dangerous

Early history speaks to us in the remote and fragmented language of bones, shards, tools, and burial mounds. The archaeological history of life on earth reaches farther back than written records. Bones are still being consulted by forensic investigators and remains of eminent citizens of Verona are being exhumed and analyzed more than six hundred years after their owners drew their final breaths. Furthermore, ancient documents were often devoted to the perils faced in the journey of the dead. Rituals for guiding and communicating with the dead have been at the core of virtually all world cultures. It has been suggested that the spiritual health of a society can be evaluated by the vigor with which it continues to perform its obligations to the dead. Something crucial to the survival of a society is endangered when the living are unwilling or unable to continue customs and rituals intended to regulate relationships with the dead.

Through the millennia, our ancestors performed rituals both to affirm communal bonds among the living and to secure the goodwill of the resident deities. Ritual performances instructed members in their group responsibilities, celebrated life, encouraged fertility, and offered protection from malevolent forces. In this sense, funerary rites certainly were for the living—but that was only part of the story. Funerals were for the dead, too. An outsider with a sharp pencil and a notebook might insist on separating and classifying societal practices, including the "for the living," and "for the dead." The society itself, though, was more likely to regard all these beliefs and processes as integrated within its worldview. From the insider's perspective it was obvious that the living needed to do right by the dead. Failure to carry through with postmortem obligations could provoke the wrath of the deceased as well as the gods. Moreover, the discontented dead were not only dangerous—they were also vulnerable, needing the help of the living community. Everybody—living and dead—was in it together.

The living had two persuasive reasons for taking good care of their dead: love and fear. Although the details of mourning customs have varied widely, people everywhere have generally sorrowed at the loss of a person dear to them. We would recognize the anguish of newly bereaved people thousands of years ago and they would recognize ours:

- We would both want to feel that our loved one is "all right," even though dead.

- We would not feel ready to sever our ties completely. There seems to be a powerful need for what has become known in recent years as "continuing bonds."

- And we would want—somehow—to continue to express our love and respect, and to keep something of that person with us.

Today, a widow might not choose to convert her husband's jawbone into a necklace or his skull into a lime-pot, but this worked for the Trobriand Islanders as they preserved and transformed anatomical artifacts to serve as generational hand-me-downs in memory of those who had come before. Perhaps the islanders would have made DVDs from the family album had this technology been available—or perhaps the "real thing" was to be preferred in any event. Whatever the particular practice, the living could not rest easy until the departed spirits were likewise settled into their spiritual or symbolic estate.

The living can move ahead confidently with their lives only after they have succeeded in helping the newly dead to attain their own kind of peace.

The vulnerability of the newly dead and their potential for malignant intervention is the side of this story that has been shooshed aside by technologically advanced societies. That the dead have something to fear and that we have something to fear from the dead might be dismissed as outmoded superstition. Nevertheless, by whatever name, fear for and of the dead continues to beset many people even if such fear is less recognized by mainstream society. It is still a powerful force within some ethnic traditions and also an impulse that can break through into the lives of mainstream people when they least expect it.

Victims of Bad Deaths

The Tohono O'odham of the American Southwest are among the many traditional societies that became outcasts in their own land. A desperate economic situation added to their plight when local employment opportunities fell victim to technological and expansionist change. The most shattering consequence has been the increased frequency of "unnatural deaths" among young males. The official causes of death are (often alcohol-related) suicide, accidents, and homicide. These deaths are disturbing for both personal and cosmic reasons. Those who die before their time are mourned by family and community, who also fear for the future of their hard-pressed society with so many losses among the younger generation. There is another ominous facet to these deaths, however. The young men died before their spirits were prepared for the transition to the next life. This untimely occurrence upsets the natural order of things. It also constitutes a threat to the community because spirits of the deceased like to visit their living family members with a kind and loving attitude. Those who have died "unnaturally" are dangerous visitors.

[Anthropologist David] Kozak found that

> To counteract this danger, the living erect death-memorials so that the soul of a "bad" death victim will return to the location of their demise, rather than to their previous, worldly existence . . . But the death-memorial is also the location where family and friends of the deceased go to assist the soul to *si' alig weco*. This term means "beyond the eastern horizon," and it is where all O'odham souls reside after death.

Funerals Are for the Living and the Dead

Here's the key point: The living can move ahead confidently with their lives only after they have succeeded in helping the newly dead to attain their own kind of peace "beyond the eastern horizon." Funerals and memorials clearly are for the living *and* the dead.

Families who had lost a member in the September 11 disaster felt they could not really start to go on with their lives until the dead had been "brought home."

Horrible nightmares have afflicted people in many times and places when they have failed to assist the dead in their passage to the next life. It's the difference between a comforting visit from the spirit of a deceased loved one and the uneasy sense of being haunted. An example of epic proportions occurred during the prime killing years of the Black Death in fourteenth-century North Africa, Asia, and Europe. The dead sometimes outnumbered the living, who, frightened and struggling for their own survival, often had to forgo ritual and dump bodies into large burial pits or crowded shallow graves. Survivor stress included the fear that their own souls had been condemned for the failure to provide the proper rituals and services. It is even possible that the fourteenth century's intensified violence and episodes of mass psychotic behavior owed something to this violation of the implicit contract between the living and the dead.

The Example of September 11

The abundant examples in our own time include the repeated television images of "first responders" to the attacks on the World Trade Center on September 11, 2001, as they worked desperately, first to rescue living victims and then to uncover human remains in Ground Zero rubble. Few would have difficulty in understanding the urgent (and, unfortunately, unrewarded) efforts at rescue. The great determination to recover the dead, however, was probably instructive to a public that had become accustomed to a more pragmatic and functionalistic approach. The assumption that "the dead are just dead" was forcefully contradicted. The victims were no longer alive, but they were not yet "safely dead," if the phrase be permitted. Both the victims and their families were in a kind of a limbo—actually, in a *limbic* zone between one identity and another. Rites-of-passage theory conceives of life as a sequence of many smaller journeys within the larger tour of the total course of existence. The theory often emphasizes the vulnerability of people who have moved from their previous secure status but have not yet reached their next destination or haven.

Both the September 11 victims and the stricken families were trapped in this nowhere zone, and there was no certain endpoint at which this painful situation would be resolved. Families who had lost a member in the September 11 disaster felt they could not really start to go on with their lives until the dead had been "brought home" in some meaningful sense of the term. Funeral and memorial services eventually were held without the bodies when it became clear that the remains would never be recovered and identified. In these and many other instances, the living have expressed their need to do all that should and could be done for the dead. For the living really to get back to life (as best they could) required that the dead also be given the opportunity to move securely to their destination on time's relentless caravan. Such circumstances illustrate how simplistic it would be to insist that funerals were either just for the living or the dead.

Are the Dead Merely Inconvenient?

In our times, the "why funerals?" question is sometimes prompted by a feeling that the dead have become an inconvenience. Funerals are merely vestigial rites that drain our precious time, money, and energy. Funerals are usually depressing affairs anyway, not that much help even to the living. We can hardly wait until they are over and then the dead are still dead, so what's been accomplished?

This view does not yet seem to be dominant in North American society but has become increasingly evident since our transformation from an agrarian nation in which most people stayed pretty much in place and the church was a cornerstone of communal life. "Deathways" have moved slowly and reluctantly along with the times as we have become a technologically enhanced land where change of address, job, and partner have become normative. Furthermore, along with other developed nations, we have achieved a significantly longer average life expectancy. Funerals less often become a gathering for sorrowing parents as their young children are laid to rest; more often the mourners are adult children who are paying their respects to a long-lived parent.

Funerals traditionally have provided both an endpoint and a starting point.

Generational Differences

There are also signs of generational differences in the importance attached to funerals and memorial services. People still make sentimental journeys to visit family burial places. With disconcerting frequency, however, the remembered neighborhoods of their childhood have been altered beyond recognition or acceptance. Many burial places, whether in churchyards, woodland fields, or town cemeteries, have deteriorated for lack of upkeep, or have even been obliterated by the forces of change. It is understandable that some family members would rather keep their memories than face such sad prospects. The dazzling phenomenon of Americans in motion has dispersed many families who "in the old days" would have been regularly popping into each other's kitchens on a regular basis. Many families do remain emotionally connected and take advantage of up-to-date communication technology. Nevertheless, it is often a physical and financial strain to travel to bedside and funeral. Studies have suggested that older adults tend to find more comfort and meaning in funerals, but it is an open question whether "the new aged" of each generation will continue to find as much value. Even years ago I would often hear from elders that it would be a shame to waste money on "funeral stuff." One of the unforgettable comments came from the resident of a geriatric hospital:

> You come here and everybody thinks you're already dead. Tell the truth: I knew I was near dead before. Every time you walk in a store and wait and nobody sees you. . . . Just

being old is just almost like being dead. Then, here. Then, dead. Who's going to care? Make a fuss? Not them. Not me.

We can hardly be surprised if people socialized within a gerophobic [fear of old age] society should themselves internalize negative attitudes and decide that their deaths as well as their lives are undeserving of attention. Others, though, rally against the ageism and try to secure a dignified and appropriate funeral for themselves. The depressive surrender and the anxious seeking are differential responses to the same underlying concern: that a long life will receive an exit stamp of "Invalid: Discard. Shelf life expired."

Funerals traditionally have provided both an endpoint and a starting point. The passage from life to death is certified as complete, so the survivors now can turn to their recovery and renewal. The effectiveness of funerals to achieve this bridging purpose can be compromised, however, by some characteristics of our times. For example, many folkways involved intensive family participation in preparing the body and the funeral arrangements (isolated examples still exist). In general, though, the preparation phase has passed to the funeral industry with the result that family mourners less often have the complete sense of release because of their limited involvement before the funeral. Furthermore, rapid socio-technological change has reduced intergenerational consensus on the value of the funeral process. One cannot assume that multiple-generation families will share priorities and expectations.

Funerals for the Nonreligious

Another challenge to the social and spiritual value of funerals has been intensifying in recent years. [Researchers] report an increase in the frequency of "funerals of the unaffiliated." More than a third of the U.S. population do not claim membership in a religious congregation. Religious officials confirm that they are being called upon more often to participate in such funerals in which families request that the religious service be "toned down."

I have noticed a parallel trend that might be called "funerals of the disengaged." People who have outlived—or, over time, drifted away from—their personal support systems are more likely to receive only perfunctory services. Those who would have felt a strong emotional link or at least a powerful sense of obligation have already passed from that person's life. People who have lived essentially solitary lives or become institutional residents have a high probability of exiting this life through the back door with minimal attention. Such an exit was a frequent occurrence within institutional settings where many residents seemed to have been forgotten or disregarded by the larger community and the facility itself was locked into a death-avoidance pattern. A funeral process that does not celebrate the life, mourn the passing, or provide symbolic safe passage through the journey of the dead—what else can we expect when the individual has been progressively disvalued through the years?

People who are uncomfortable with the familiar words, symbols, and gestures of mainstream religion are nevertheless finding ways to incorporate spiritual considerations into the funeral process.

It is understandable that funerals might be disvalued if they seem to have lost their inner connection to the values and meanings that guide our lives. It is that inner connection that makes a difference between empty ritual and participation in an event that is both universal and deeply personal. To ask, "Why funerals?" may sound like a rejection of the whole process. Most often, though, the question expresses a search for renewal of the inner connection between how we live and how we die.

New Funeral Rituals

That search is now taking a variety of forms. People who are uncomfortable with the familiar words, symbols, and gestures of mainstream religion are nevertheless finding ways to incorporate spiritual considerations into the funeral process. The "postmodern funeral" may include such elements as a candle-lighting ceremony and improvised memorials, music, and eulogies that are somehow special to the particular people involved. New partnerships are developing between those funeral directors who are open to change and those families who are determined that the funeral process represent their own way of life.

Two very different pathways are among those being explored. Some people are exploring the potentials of virtual funerals and memorials on the Internet—often as a supplement to a more conventional service. Others are turning to "green funerals." These are burials in woodland areas that are intended to return the body to earth in a natural form. There is no embalming to leak chemicals into the ground, and simple, biodegradable materials are used, e.g., willow coffins. Funerals are to be removed from the technological-commercial matrix and put in the service of "producing wildlife habitats and forests from green burial sites, where native trees, wildflowers and protected animals are encouraged ... meadow brown butterfly colonies, grasshoppers, insects, bats, voles and owls to multiply ... where the mechanical mower does not prey on a regular basis and a self-supporting ecosystem can evolve."

We can recognize that the funeral process offers an opportunity to reach deep into our understanding and values.

The funeral process today is caught up within the broader matrix of social change. Some of the negatives have already been identified. To these must be added that narrow construction of human life that embraces youth and material success but recoils from the specter of loss and limits. Where this attitudinal climate prevails, it is tempting to reject funerals because we are exposed there to the uncomfortable reminders of aging and death. Nevertheless, it remains as true today as ever that "taking good care of the dead" is a vital part of a society's support for the living. [Forensic anthropologist] Clea Koff, "The Bone Woman," has demonstrated this fact again as she contributed to the healing process in Rwanda by honoring the remains of the massacre victims.

Funerals Help Us Understand Life

Yes, funerals can take the form of dysfunctional vestiges if we let them go that way. Another choice is available to us, though. We can recognize that the funeral process offers an opportunity to reach deep into our understanding and values. Perhaps our society today does not offer the clearest and firmest guide to comprehension of life and death. Perhaps it is up to us, then, to review our own beliefs about the meanings of growth and loss, youth and age, life and death—and to listen carefully to the beliefs of those to whom we offer service.

8

Contemporary Funerals Do Not Adequately Honor the Dead

John Fraser

John Fraser writes for Maclean's *magazine, a popular Canadian periodical.*

Contemporary practices including obituaries and funerals no longer treat the dead with respect, although the funeral industry has grown dramatically. Newspapers looking to increase revenues encourage families to write long and maudlin obituaries. In addition, funeral eulogies often focus more on the person giving the eulogy than on the dead person. Contemporary funerals are often framed as a "celebration of life," rather than offering mourners the opportunity of reflecting on their own mortality. Because contemporary funeral practices obscure the reality of death, they do not adequately honor the dead.

"Death be not proud, though some have called thee mighty and dreadful," wrote John Donne, the 17th-century Anglican divine who was also one of the great metaphysical poets of his day. "Thy mouth was open," added Donne's colleague George Herbert in another direct address to Death, "but thou coulds't not sing . . ."

Ha! Old Death is standing tall these days, belting out new songs like a torch singer and generally thinking pretty big

John Fraser, "The Way We Mourn: Obit Notices Are Epic and Funeral Services Are Overblown, But Death Itself Is Nowhere to Be Found," *Maclean's*, vol. 120, September 3, 2007, pp. 50–52. Copyright © 2007 by *Maclean's* Magazine. Reproduced by permission.

things, at least if Canadian funerals and the attendant folderol that afflicts the recently departed is anything to go by. The "Simple Alternative" may be there for the discerning few who want to avoid all the extremities of expenses death can bring upon a grieving family, but the business of death continues to expand, although today there is a new twist to the end of life—it doesn't have to happen.

The Reality of Death Is Obscured Today

Or so it seems sometimes. First of all, the word itself—Death—is a major no-no. It's a downer and suggests earthly finality—or finality, period. As the Age of Faith makes its final, fitful departure and disappears beneath the Western Sea, and along with it the confidence in an afterlife, the reality of death has been increasingly and perversely obscured. Death goes against the spirit of the age. It's not on the agenda. It is almost politically incorrect.

Conveniently, you don't actually have to die anymore, at least not linguistically. Just read the funeral announcements in any newspaper on any given day. At the most, people simply disappear "suddenly" or "peacefully" or "courageously" or "quietly" or "unexpectedly." Of the 24 departed ones who "slipped" or "passed" away on a recent Tuesday in July in the columns of the *Globe and Mail* [Canadian newspaper], apparently only four actually "died." All the rest entered a euphemistic Valhalla [the Viking site of the afterlife] encumbered only by a genial shroud of feel-good adjectives.

The Contemporary Obituary

And that's just the beginning of the subterfuge, the big denial. It's not entirely clear how it all got started, but some time during the past decade many North American newspaper ad managers discovered that the lineage for death announcements could be dramatically increased if the bereaved survivors were encouraged, by hook or by crook, to fatten up the tales of the departed ones. If the famous could always get their life stories, gilded and buffed to a high polish, splashed across a newspaper page in 12-point type with accompanying pictures, the hoi polloi were suddenly offered the same transformative experience for their loved ones in egalitarian agate 8-point type at incrementally increased costs by the line. The pictures obviously were an add-on and cost extra. What was once a terse gazetteer announcement to neighbours and interested associates has now turned into an epic saga for the benefit of ... well, it's not entirely clear: perhaps the egos of the surviving family members.

Anybody who follows the death announcements (and that means most people over a certain age) can cite examples of announcements so over the top they almost reach Pluto.

Here is a recent example, with names and certain details changed in order not to inadvertently hurt the feelings of a well-intentioned family which has nevertheless trod upon territory the English satirist Evelyn Waugh, author of *The Loved One*, would have relished:

ANGLETON, Amy Bessborough (née Pentworth)—Suddenly but peacefully, without a word of complaint, on Friday May 8th. After a rich and vibrant life, Amy leaves indelible memories to her beloved son John and her daughters Ruth Kelso and Kristy Ann, as well as her seven wonderful grandchildren. We will celebrate Amy's beautiful life at a special service of thanksgiving on Wednesday, May 13th at the Banks of Jordan Funeral Home. Amy came to Montreal in 1927 with her parents after an early childhood in Chatham, Ont. In Montreal, she attended Miss Fairbank's Academy and won medals in everything she tried out for, although she was best remembered for starting the first bridge club at the school (the Amy Pentworth Cup is still competed for). A strikingly pretty woman, Amy reached full maturity set against all the drama of World War II, where she played her part in the war effort as a nurse's aide. It was during these years, so fondly recalled ever afterwards, that Amy met the father of her children and although the marriage was tragically cut short by the heartbreak of a cruel mental disease, Amy's indomitable spirit reigned supreme. In particular, her son John remembers her courage during this period when she was beset by both financial worries and the "challenge" of exuberant teenagers. Bridge sustained her spirits throughout these and later years and her special friends Ruth Danton and Ethel Jackson will be missing her greatly. Sadly, her final days were afflicted with Alzheimer's, although she always retained her great dignity of bearing. In lieu of flowers, Amy's family would be grateful if donations could be sent to the Fairbank's Academy in Montreal or the Alzheimer's Society of Canada.

And this actually is a quite gentle announcement, somewhat restrained, and half the length of some of the sagas that now appear daily in newspapers at considerable cost to the bereaved. Anybody who follows the death announcements (and that means most people over a certain age) can cite examples of announcements so far over the top they almost reach Pluto.

One particularly memorable instance was of a society lady in Western Canada who shot her husband in his legs after she caught him philandering, went on to be arrested, tried and imprisoned, and then emerged back into her somewhat more restrained but affluent social life of volunteer service, bridge nights and birthday parties with the grandchildren. At the time of the shooting, it was a big national news story, but her survivors, in the subsequent death announcement a few years later, merely alluded to "mom's unfortunate difficulties"— three little words in an essay of Horatian dimensions reciting all of mom's achievements.

The Contemporary Eulogy

Another syndrome that has infected the business of death is the self-important, self-serving eulogy. Some people just cannot pay tribute to a dead person without overlaying everything with their own story. The greatness of the departed one is weighed mostly in the balance of the larger greatness of the eulogist. Usually this is simply pompous; sometimes, though, it can be quite comical. When the late and great journalist and social activist June Callwood died [in 2007], there was understandably an outpouring from fellow scribes. The most cringemalting, though, came from the *Globe and Mail's* television critic, John Doyle, the whole point of which was to quote a letter Callwood had once sent him congratulating him on a particular piece and for improving "the craft" of writing.

Most commemorations are bodiless and rendered in the bleak pseudo-ecclesiastical meeting rooms of funeral parlours.

You could see the same syndrome at work after the death of Richard Bradshaw, the brilliant opera magician who built Canada's first opera house and made the Canadian Opera Company a world leader. Here's the distinguished German-Canadian tenor Michael Schade writing of his terrible grief in the *Globe and Mail's* letter page. I'll just quote the first paragraph to give you the gist. Note the nine times "I" and "me" are used versus the five times for "he" and "him":

As I am sitting here at the Salzburg Festival for the 14th consecutive summer, I am remembering Richard Bradshaw and raising a glass in his honour. I wouldn't be here without him—his faith in me as a young singer and his encouragement gave me the confidence to pursue this wonderful, crazy life. When Richard cast me as Oedipus Rex, I don't think either of us expected how key a role this would play in our lives. For Richard, it confirmed the adventurous path he had chosen for the Canadian Opera Company; for me, it was a personal triumph and a great leap forward in my career.

The Contemporary Funeral

Although death is almost always infinitely sad for those immediately affected, these often twittering announcements and self-serving eulogies are merely emblematic decoration to a much deeper cover-up that has emerged over the past few years, in funerals themselves. It is rare now for a dead body to be served up at a "funeral." Most commemorations are bodiless and rendered in the bleak pseudo-ecclesiastical meeting rooms of funeral parlours. If a service is held at a church, it is almost invariably a "service of thanksgiving," or "a celebration." Even here, the presence of the recently departed is an increasingly rare event. Nothing, it seems, is more unwelcome at a funeral these days than The Corpse.

If a traditional funeral is held, it is often disconcerting or considered eccentric, even anti-social. This week in Toronto, for example, Richard Bradshaw was buried with astringent solemnities at Toronto's St. James' Cathedral that left many people shaking their heads at its harrowing simplicity. Not only were there no operatic histrionics, there was no parade of favourite memories, no touchy-feely hymns and poems, no fond and amusing anecdotes to give us some comic relief from the tragedy of a life cut short from further promise.

The mood of the times demands that the dead be celebrated, not mourned; made present instead of departed; reborn in verbiage rather than buried in a shroud.

It was reminiscent of the much smaller funeral, in May 2005, for the Canadian author and journalist Christina Mc-Call. Her family walked her body down the aisle and their grief was palpable. Unlike Richard Bradshaw, Ms. McCall had been ill for some time, but in both cases these were clearly incredibly difficult and sad departures. The centuries-old Book of Common Prayer service, which focuses on the hope of redemption, salvation and resurrection, was directed in both cases at everyone at the funeral. While this obviously included Bradshaw and McCall (God is reminded, among other things, that each of these two—like everyone else present—was "a sinner of your own making"), the traditional obsequies and observances for the dead in the long Judeo-Christian tradition manifestly focus on the living and the ordeals still to be borne before our own deaths and hopes of salvation.

A Mixed Response

What was curious about the McCall and Bradshaw services was how they divided those who attended. In McCall's case, for example, no eulogies from family members or friends and associates were made and, as a priest explained before the service, only the church's traditional reminders that we sprang from dust and end up as dust would accompany Christina McCall's passage from this world to the next. The attendant solemn liturgy was exclusively designed not to individually immortalize someone who was already immortalized, but to remind those of us "left behind" that our own lives were as transient as the one whose death we were grieving. "Brief life is here our portion," the hymn goes, "brief sorrow, short-lived care."

For many, it was a moving, solemn and beautifully spiritual farewell, imbued with tragedy, acceptance and the remission of earthly grief in anticipation of another life totally beyond mortal knowledge and assurance. This evidently resonated for Christina McCall, because it was the service she asked for, and also for her immediate family. But the verdict was not unanimous.

Reading a column by McCall's former associate, Allan Fotheringham, or her former husband, Peter C. Newman, a few days later, you would have thought a major act of sacrilege had been committed. Both men wanted to hear all about the achievements of her life trotted out for one last airing before internment, as if anyone who was at the funeral didn't know what he or she was doing there. Fotheringham even saw in the spare and elegiac service all the proof needed to understand why mainstream churches are in decline. The service had made no concessions to the mood of the times, and the mood of the times demands that the dead be celebrated, not mourned; made present instead of departed; reborn in verbiage rather than buried in a shroud.

There's something else lost [in contemporary funerals] . . . and that is that Death itself is largely diminished in all the hoopla.

This syndrome, I feel, can be laid at the feet of two famous ladies, one "departed" but far from gone, and the other very much still with us: Diana and Oprah. When the masses applauded the appalling eulogy Princess Diana's lounge lizard of a brother, Earl Spencer, made in Westminster Abbey, you knew, you just knew, something major had changed in group sensitivities. And if you didn't know it from that fateful day, you can tune in daily to Oprah to understand that everyone now, in theory, has the right to splatter their lives over the public airwaves, regardless of how banal, sentimental, embarrassing or irrelevant it may be to the larger world. If you have not yet had your Warholian 15 minutes of fame, let not your spirit be troubled: your family and executors will make sure it comes at the end.

What's wrong with a stylized funeral that serves the emotional needs of the immediate families and friends? Nothing, I suppose, except the loss of a certain decent reticence and restraint in the face of this awe-ful reality. Reticence and restraint are not part of the age, certainly. But there's something else lost, too, which is more difficult to explain and that is that Death itself is largely diminished in all the hoopla. Our grandparents understood death so much better than we do. They understood its arbitrariness through disease, poverty and war. They understood the particular tragedy of the young dying, from any cause; they also understood the beauty of death coming after a long life well lived.

Many eulogists end up talking about themselves rather than the Departed One.

The traditional liturgy of all denominations and all religions underscores the transient nature of life, the gratitude for the privilege of having been able to spend time on earth, and, for those with curiosity about the spiritual dimension of life, the hope of an existence beyond the earthly grave. At the root of traditional liturgy is the fear of God, which is to say an acceptance that there is something so much larger than anything we can actually imagine at work in the universe. In this sense, even though death is a big event for the immediately bereaved, it is a tiny blip in the history of the cosmos and to imagine it as something bigger is an act of ego.

The "Celebration of Life" Syndrome Is Not Appropriate

This is the opposite of the "celebration of life" syndrome of most funerals these days, the kind the disappointed mourners at McCall's funeral wanted, the kind that start to sound like an Oprah symposium of being positive about bad news events. The fact that so many eulogists end up talking about themselves rather than the Departed One is actually part of the package: personal fulfillment being a key component in the obsequies of our times.

When the novelist Robertson Davies died in 1995, he had left word that he wanted an ordinary service from the Book of Common Prayer in a college chapel—no Homily—and with the chaplain of the day presiding. A few days later, because he was a considerable public figure, over 1,000 people turned up at the University of Toronto's huge Convocation Hall to hear a whole slew of wonderful accounts of his life. In his case it was appropriate. In the case of the less famous, the traditional wake or reception following a funeral service was a good time for a few well-chosen words from close friends and associates. But this tradition, too, is dying because people seem to want starring roles. I have attended "celebrations" in which the eulogists, like Michael Schade and John Doyle, simply forgot whom they were celebrating as they recited their own interesting journeys through life. It is [an exaggeration] of death as well as an often unwitting denial of the power of death in our lives.

"No man is an island," John Donne also wrote. "Any man's death diminishes me because I am a part of the whole. Therefore ask not for whom the bell tolls, it tolls for thee." Yes, for thee and me, and the ad director of the death columns, and the funeral home folks, and all the chatty company of the non-dead, the never-dying, the eulogists and the not-gone-but-departed. And while we're at it, let's hear the story again about how you and dear old X "fished together as boys and I discovered that my destiny was to be in bio-tech and that's how I made my name and my first mill . . ."

Requiescat in pace [rest in peace] . . . but where and when and how on earth?

9

Contemporary Funerals Should Include the Body

Thomas Lynch

Thomas Lynch is the author of several books of poetry and essays, including The Undertaking: Life Studies in the Dismal Trade *(1997) and* Bodies in Motion and at Rest: On Metaphor and Mortality *(2001). He is a funeral director in Milford, Michigan.*

While most people can agree about what constitutes a "good" death and "good" grief, there is significant disagreement about the components of a good funeral. Contemporary clergy and laity seem to be moving toward memorial services that do not include the dead body because it is more convenient for everyone. However, because human beings are both body and soul, it is important to care for the body in death as in life. Consequently, good funerals are ones in which the bodies of the dead are present and treated with respect.

It's sunny and 70 at Chapel Hill. I'm speaking to Project Compassion, an advocacy group for end-of-life issues, on an unlikely trinity of oxymorons—the *good* death, *good* grief and the *good* funeral. "What," most people reasonably ask, "can ever be good about death or grief or funerals?" The 130 people in this room understand. They are mostly women—clergy, hospice and social workers, doctors, nurses and funeral directors—and they work, so to speak, in the deep end of the pool, with the dying, the dead and the bereaved.

What Is a Good Death?

We begin by agreeing that the good death is the one that happens when we are among our own, surrounded not by beeping meters and blinking monitors but by the faces of family and people who care. It is the death of a whole person, not an ailing part. It is neither a failure nor an anomaly; it is less science and more serenity. The good death, like the good life, does not happen in isolation. It is not only or entirely a medical event, nor only or entirely a social or spiritual or retail one. The good death engages our entire humanity—both what is permanent and what is passing. So I am thanking these women for the power of their presence—as nurses and doctors and hospice volunteers, as pastors and rabbis, priests and imams, as mothers and daughters, sisters and wives—for their willingness to stand in the room where someone is dying, without an easy answer, without a cure or false hopes, with only their own humanity to bear witness and to be present. The power of being there is that it emboldens others—family and friends—to be present too to the glorious and sorrowful mysteries.

We deal with death by dealing with the dead, not just the idea but also the sad and actual fact of the matter— the dead body.

And grief, *good* grief we further concur, is something about which we have little choice. It is the tax we pay on the loves of our lives, our habits and attachments. And like every other tax there is this dull math to it—if you love, you grieve. So the question is not so much whether or not, but rather how well, how completely, how meaningfully we mourn. And though we do not grieve as those who have no faith grieve, as people of faith we grieve nonetheless. We talk about the deeper meanings we sometimes find in the contemplation of these things and how we sometimes feel God's presence there, and sometimes God's absence.

And everything is going very well. We are all nodding in warm consensus. It's like preaching to the choir—until I come to the part where I talk about a *good* funeral.

The Good Funeral

A good funeral, I tell them, serves the living by caring for the dead. It tends to both—the living and dead—because a death in the family happens to both. A good funeral transports the newly deceased and the newly bereaved to the borders of a changed reality. The dead are disposed of in a way that says they mattered to us, and the living are brought to the edge of a life they will lead without the one who has died. We deal with death by dealing with the dead, not just the idea but also the sad and actual fact of the matter—the dead body.

Here is where some of the audience stops nodding. Brows furrow, eyes narrow into squints, as if something doesn't exactly compute. The idea of death is one thing. A dead body is quite another. An Episcopal priest in the third row raises her hand [to] ask "Why do we need the body there? Isn't it, after all, just a shell?" She is speaking, she tells me, from a Christian perspective.

The "Just a Shell" Theory

This "just a shell" theory is a favorite among clergy of my generation. Their pastoral educations on death and bereavement began and, for many of them, ended with *The American Way of Death*—Jessica Mitford's 1983 best-selling lampoon of funerals and funeral directors. It was an easy and often hilarious read. Mitford made much of the math of caskets—how much they cost, how profitable they were, how devious or obsequious the sales pitch was. She disliked the boxes for their expense. And she disliked the bodies in the boxes for the untidy and unpredictable feelings that surrounded them. She recommended getting rid of both caskets and corpses, and letting convenience and cost efficiency replace what she regarded as pricey and barbaric display.

The bodies of Mitford's first husband, who died in the war; her first daughter, who died in infancy; and her first son, who was killed by a bus in Berkeley, California, all "disappeared"—dispatched without witness or rubric and never mentioned in *The American Way of Death* nor in two volumes of autobiography. Their names were erased from the books of her life for fear of the feelings that might linger there. Fearful that the sight of a dead body might trigger overwhelming emotions, she down-sized it to "just a shell" to be burned or buried without attendant bother or much expense.

This was a welcome notion among many of the clergy coming of age in the latter decades of the last century. It aligned nicely with their sense that, just as merchants were removing Christ from Christmas, morticians were removing faith from funerals. What need have Christians of all this bother—caskets, flowers, wakes and processions. Aren't the sureties of heaven enough? The "just a shell" theory furthermore articulated the differences between the earthly and heavenly, the corruptible and incorruptible, the base and blessed, sacred and profane, sinful natures and holy spirits.

Bodies and Soul

Human beings are bodies and souls. And souls, made in the image and likeness of God, are eternal and essential, whereas bodies are mortal and impermanent. "There is," the scripture holds, "a natural body and a spiritual body." In life, we are regarded as one—a whole being, body and soul, flesh and blood and spirit. And we are charged with the care and maintenance of both. We feed the flesh and the essence. We pamper the wounds and strive to improve the condition of both body and soul. We read and run wind sprints, we fast and pray, confide in our pastors and medicos, and seek communion, spiritual and physical, with other members of our species. "Know ye not," Paul asks the Corinthians, "that ye are the temple of God, and that the Spirit of God dwelleth in you?"

The eventual [memorial] "celebration" will be a lovely and, needless to say, "life-affirming" event to which everyone is invited—except, of course, the one who has died.

But in death, the good priest in the third row seemed to be saying, the temple becomes suddenly devalued, suddenly irrelevant, suddenly negligible and disposable—"just a shell" from which we ought to seek a hurried and most often unseen riddance.

The Inconvenience of the Body

Like many of her fellow clergy she finds the spiritual bodies more agreeable than the natural ones. The spirits are well intentioned and faultless; the bodies are hungry, lustful, greedy and weak. The soul is the sanctuary of faith, the body full of doubts and despairs. The soul sees the straight and narrow path, whereas the body wants the easier, softer way. The corruptible bleeds and belches and dies, and the incorruptible is perfect and perpetual. Souls are just easier all around. Which is why for years she's been officiating at memorial services instead of funerals. They are easier, more convenient and more cost-efficient. They are notable for their user-friendliness. They can be scheduled around the churches' priorities—the day care and Stephen Ministries, the Bible studies and rummage sales—and around a pastor's all-too-busy schedule. A quick and private disposal of the dead removes the sense of emergency and immediacy from a death in the family. . . .

There is no bother with coffins at all. The dead are secreted off to the crematory or grave while the living go about their business. Where a dead body requires more or less immediate attention, riddance of "just the shell" can hold grief off for a few days, or a week, or a season, No cutting short the pastor's too brief vacation, no rushing home from a ministerial conference to deal with a death in the parish family. The eventual "celebration" will be a lovely and, needless to say, "life-affirming" event to which everyone is invited—except, of course, the one who has died. The talk is determinedly uplifting, the finger food and memorabilia are all in good taste, the music more purposefully cheering than poignant, the bereaved most likely on their best behavior, less likely to "break down," "fall apart" or "go to pieces"—they will be brave and faithful. And "closure," if not achieved, is nonetheless proclaimed, often just before the Merlot runs out.

Memorial Services Refuse to Deal with the Dead

The memorial service makes much of dealing with memories of the dead by steadfastly refusing to deal with the dead themselves. It is the emotional and commemorative equivalent of a baptism without the baby or a wedding without the blushing bride or a graduation without the graduates. A funeral without the dead body has the religious significance of the Book of Job without the sores and boils, Exodus without the stench of frogs, Calvary without a cross, or the cross without the broken, breathless, precious body hanging there, all suffering and salvation. It is Easter without the resurrected body.

The funeral ... must deal with our humanity and our Christianity, our spiritual and natural realities, our flesh, our fears, our faith and hopes, our bodies and our souls.

So I asked her reverence: What if her congregants, instead of showing up to worship, left "just their shells" in bed on Sunday mornings? Or what if, instead of dressing up the children's "shells" and driving them across town to church, they assured their pastor that they were "with her in spirit"? Might she think there was something missing from the morning services? At this she looked at me, perplexed. Or what if Jesus had not raised his "just a shell" from the dead? What if he'd resurrected the "Idea" of himself, say, or his personality? Would we all be Christians these centuries since?

The clergywoman was not amused.

When Joseph of Arimathea, in league with Nicodemus, pleaded with Pilate for "just" the body of Christ, he was acting out a signature duty of our species. And when the Marys came bearing spices and ointments to anoint the corpse, they too were acting out longstanding obsequies "in keeping with the customs of the Jews." It is the custom of humankind to deal with death by dealing with the dead.

The defining truth of our Christianity—an empty tomb—proceeds from the defining truth of our humanity: we fill tombs. The mystery of the resurrection to eternal life is bound inextricably to the experience of suffering and death. Indeed, the effort to make sense of life—the religious impulse—owes much to our primeval questions about the nature of death.

Is that all there is? Can it happen to me? Why is it cold? What comes next?

[The funeral] is not for dodging our dead, but for bearing us up as we bear them to the grave or tomb or fire.

The Funeral Must Be for Body and Soul

The funeral—that ritual wheel that works the space between the living and the dead—must deal with our humanity and our Christianity, our spiritual and natural realities, our flesh, our fears, our faith and hopes, our bodies and our souls.

Lately it seems the wheel is broken, or has gone off the track, or must be reinvented every day. Nowadays news of a death is often attended by a gathering ambiguity about what we ought to do about it. We have more choices and fewer certainties, more options and fewer customs. The culture—that combination of religious, ethnic, social and market dynamics—seems to have failed us. We are drawn, it seems, toward two extremes—to do anything and everything or to do nothing at all. . . .

A good funeral is not about how much we spend or how much we save. Rather it is about what we do—to act out our faith, our hopes, our loves and losses. Pastoral care is not about making death easier, or grief less keenly felt or funerals cheaper or more convenient. It is about bringing the power of faith to bear on the human experience of dying, death and bereavement. And our faith is not for getting around grief or past it, but for getting through it. It is not for denying death, but for confronting it. It is not for dodging our dead, but for bearing us up as we bear them to the grave or tomb or fire at the edge of which we give them back to God.

Caring for the Body

Among the several blessings of my work as a funeral director is that I have seen the power of such faith in the face of death. I remember the churchman at the deathbed of a neighbor—it was four in the morning in the middle of winter—who gathered the family around to pray, then helped me guide the stretcher through the snow out to where our hearse was parked. Three days later, after the services at church, he rode with me in the hearse to the grave, committed the body with a handful of earth and then stood with the family and friends as the grave was filled, reading from the psalms—the calm in his voice and the assurance of the words making the sad and honorable duties bearable.

I remember the priest I called to bury one of our town's indigents—a man without family or friends or finances. He, the gravediggers and I carried the casket to the grave. The priest incensed the body blessed it with holy water and read from the liturgy for 20 minutes, then sang *In Paradisum*—that gorgeous Latin for "May the angels lead you into Paradise"—as we lowered the poor man's body into the ground. When I asked him why he'd gone to such trouble he said these are the most important funerals—even if only God is watching—because it affirms the agreement between "all God's children" that we will witness and remember and take care of each other.

And I remember the Presbyterian pastor, a woman of strength and compassion who assisted a young mother whose baby had died in placing the infant's body into a tiny casket. She held the young woman as she placed a cross in the baby's hands and a teddy bear at the baby's side and then, because the mother couldn't, the pastor carefully closed the casket lid. They stood and prayed together—"God grant us the serenity to accept the things we cannot change"—then drove with me to the crematory.

Or the Baptist preacher called to preach the funeral of one of our famously imperfect citizens who drank and smoked and ran a little wild, contrary to how his born-again parents had raised him. Instead of damnation and altar calls, the pastor turned the service into a lesson in God's love and mercy and forgiveness. After speaking about the man's Christian youth, he allowed as how he had "gone astray" after he'd left home and joined the army. "It seems he couldn't keep his body and his soul aligned," the young pastor said, and seemed a little lost for words until he left the pulpit, walked over and opened the casket, took out a harmonica and began to play "Just As I Am" while everyone in the congregation nodded and wept and smiled, some of them mouthing the words of promise and comfort to themselves.

In each case these holy people treated the bodies of the dead neither as a bother or embarrassment, nor an idol or icon, nor just a shell. They treated the dead like one of our own, precious to the people who loved them, temples of the Holy Spirit, neighbors, family, fellow pilgrims. They stand— these local heroes, these saints and sinners, these men and women of God—in that difficult space between the living and the dead, between faith and fear, between humanity and Christianity and say out loud, "Behold, I show you a mystery."

10

Excarnation Is an Important Religious Tradition

Rachel Laribee

Rachel Laribee is a 2005 graduate of St. Mary's College in Maryland. She studied at Fudan University in China and traveled extensively in China and Tibet.

Tibetans practice an ancient form of body disposal known as "sky burial," or excarnation. The dead body is not preserved in any way and must sit untouched for three days before being moved to an outdoor site where more than 100 vultures wait. A monk dismembers the body and, at a signal, the vultures consume the dead flesh. While the scene might appear to be gruesome to Western outsiders, sky burial is an important cultural ritual for Tibetan Buddhists. It is a system of body disposal suited to the Tibetan terrain and climate, and one that affirms Buddhist belief in the circle of reincarnation.

We were all sitting in the back of this run-down old red truck. The feel of rusted red paint was under my fingertips. The smell of yak was in the air, but I didn't mind. I was the only Westerner among twenty monks, all riding together on this bumpy, torn up, dirt road in Tibet.

It was only a few days before this trip when I first met my "Tibetan Father." Having arrived in Lhasa [capital of Tibet] alone, I was hungry for companionship and I found it in this lovely monk outside the holy temple in Lhasa. We had only been talking a few hours before he invited me to dinner, and

Rachel Laribee, "Tibetan Sky Burial," *River Gazette*, vol. 5, no. 2, April-May 2005, p. 9. www.smcm.edu/rivergazette. Reproduced by permission.

we had been friends for several days before he invited me to travel with him and other monks to a monastery outside of Lhasa. He was fatherly toward me, and I could tell he wanted to show me something. He called me his "little Western daughter" and I called him "my Tibetan Father." The more time we spent together, the more meaningful these names truly became.

An Invitation to a Sky Burial

It took several hours to get to the small village, where we got out and hiked up a small hill to the Drigung Monastery. After we ate, I was ready to go to bed. But before I left, Father Monk asked me if I wanted to join him in the morning to watch the Tibetan Sky Burial. Knowing that this was a chance in a lifetime, I was quick to accept yet another generous offer.

Squawking and shoving each other, it took only fifteen minutes for the vultures to completely consume everything from the body, except for its skeleton.

The next morning, we exited the monastery to the east and hiked about half a mile up a hill to a rock cluster. Along with around twenty monks and a dozen Tibetan family members, I sat in a large half-circle of stones, all gathered around this large, flat boulder where the ceremony would take place. I decided to wait until everyone else sat before taking my seat. Unfortunately, the only seat left was at the bottom left part of this semicircle. On my immediate left lay an even larger boulder than the one in front of us. In that spot stood a single monk with his hand in the air, holding back 100 to 150 vultures, all about two meters in size, all squawking while watching and waiting.

An Ancient Tibetan Rite

Two men carried something large, wrapped in cloth, and placed it on the boulder in front of us. Then one of these men removed the cloth, revealing the dead, naked body of an old Tibetan man. By the awful smell and the greenish tint of the body, it was immediately apparent to me that this man had been dead for several days, and without any preservation. In fact, the Tibetan rites call for the body to remain untouched for three days, allowing for the offering of prayers and chanting.

Then a man dressed in long white aprons came, holding a large ax. Kneeling over the body, he scalped its head, removing the hair, and broke and removed the teeth. He then began to dismember the body, cutting the arms, legs, and chest into smaller pieces. The organs were removed for later disposal. When he was finished, the man stepped back about twenty feet. To the right of the vultures was another monk holding his arm out in front of the vultures. When the body was ready, he lowered his arm. At that moment, and only then, the vultures swarmed around the body and began eating its flesh. Squawking and shoving each other, it took only fifteen minutes for the vultures to completely consume everything from the body, except for its skeleton.

The term "sky burial" was coined because . . . when the vultures fly off, they spread the body to all the corners of Tibet by casting their droppings on the high mountain peaks.

The vultures immediately returned to their boulder and again waited. The man in white came back to the body, this time carrying a sledgehammer, and proceeded to shatter the skeleton of the body into pieces. When he finished, he again stepped back while the other man signaled the vultures a second time. The vultures swarmed around the shattered skeleton, this time leaving nothing.

The Vultures Do Their Best

It took about one hour from the time the body was placed to the completion of the sky burial. After the body was completely eaten, the vultures went back to their boulder. The whole process was repeated two more times, with two more dead bodies and two more feasts for the vultures. After the third body was consumed, the vultures flew off into the beautiful Tibetan sky. The term "sky burial" was coined because it is thought that when the vultures fly off, they spread the body to all the corners of Tibet by casting their droppings on the high mountain peaks.

Even though I am very familiar with the Tibetan culture and their practices, I must confess that at first, I was still dismayed that this culture that I had grown to love would treat their dead as if they were nothing more than lunch meat. But as I watched this ritual take place, I looked at the faces of the family of the deceased Tibetan man. There were no signs of horror on their faces, nor any hint of tears. The Tibetans believe that the soul and spirit of each person just borrows the body, and therefore death is just another phase in the circle of reincarnation. The sky burial is not full of mourning, for the tears and mourning are completed earlier during the three days of prayers and chants after one dies. The function of the sky burial is simply the disposal of the body.

The Cycle of Reincarnation

The cycle of reincarnation begins when the droppings enter the earth. The idea of reincarnation as a method of religious succession has been a religious belief in Tibet from the 12th century. The idea derives from the Buddhist belief that all humans are trapped in an endless sequence of birth, death, and rebirth until they achieve nirvana (enlightenment). Because the soul is reincarnated into another body, the soul never dies;

it remains in the cycle until it reaches nirvana. Therefore, death for a Tibetan is not the end, merely the beginning for a new stage in a soul's existence.

Though Tibetans practice several forms of burial rites, the sky burial is the most common method. The harsh Tibetan terrain makes the ground often too hard to dig into, and with fuel and timber scarce, the sky burial is often the best option.

As I walked back to the monastery with my "father monk," he explained to me the reasons of the sky burial. Now, not only do I understand why the Tibetans use this form of burial, but now I realize how important this ritual is for the Tibetan culture—and for that reason, this ritual has become important to me. After we reached the monastery, I thanked my father monk and bid my entire family of monks goodbye. I then began my long ride back to Lhasa, sitting in the back of yet another old, run-down truck.

11

Excarnation Is No Longer a Viable Way to Dispose of the Dead

Braden Reddall

Braden Reddall is an environmental journalist who contributes regularly to Reuters news service.

The Parsis, Indian followers of the ancient religion of Zoroastrianism, dispose of their dead through the traditional ritual of excarnation, which is the removal of flesh from a corpse by vultures. In India, however, the vulture population has plummeted due to urbanization and pollution, and there are not enough vultures to handle the number of dead placed in the "towers of silence," the location where Parsis put their dead. Although sun concentrators and chemicals have been used to hasten decomposition, without adequate vultures, excarnation is no longer a fully viable option for the disposal of the dead.

Hundreds of vultures once circled above a sacred area in one of India's poshest suburbs, waiting to feed on the remains of followers of an ancient religion that does not allow its dead to be buried or burned.

Older members of the small-but-prominent Zoroastrian Parsi community of Mumbai [India] say it usually took only half an hour for the vultures to finish their part of the ritual, cleaning a dead body of flesh deemed to be spiritually contaminated.

Pragmatism vs. Tradition

But the birds have almost been wiped out by urban development and accidental poisoning, leaving Parsis divided on how best to treat the dead and stay true to the faith.

The Parsis, long known for their philanthropy, are caught in a tug-of-war between pragmatism and tradition that goes beyond funerals to questions about conversion and racial purity.

"Our last act of charity was with the vulture," said Khojeste Mistree, a Parsi scholar. "That's the tradition that we have grown up to follow, and that tradition has come under threat.

"When you look at most cultures, the vulture's seen as a scavenger, in a very negative light, whereas to us the vulture's a religious bird because it's . . . performing a religious service."

Having fled Iran centuries ago, there are about 40,000 Parsis in Mumbai, representing more than a quarter of all Zoroastrians.

Zorastrians believe death is not just a part of life, but the temporary triumph of evil over good, which means a dead body would pollute the sacred: earth, water or fire.

They have played a formidable part in the history of India's largest city and financial capital, known as Bombay until 1995.

Prominent Parsis range from famed industrialist J.N. Tata, who built Mumbai's landmark Taj Mahal hotel, to rock star Freddie Mercury, born Farrokh Bulsara, who studied just outside the city.

The "towers of silence" or "dakhma", where Parsis place their dead, is in the Malabar Hill neighbourhood overlooking the sea, home to film stars, politicians and stock brokers, making debate about it all the more charged.

A Divided Community

Parsis also struggled to reach a consensus on other key issues, including marrying outside the faith and conversion, without which modernisers fear the religion will perish.

"The community is divided," said Minoo Shroff, chairman of the city's Parsi Punchayet, the largest community trust. "We don't have a pope here. We are guided by very many people."

Zoroastrians believe death is not just part of life, but the temporary triumph of evil over good, which means a dead body would pollute the sacred: earth, water or fire.

Cattle Drug Kills Vultures

Mistree notes this is both practical for a religion rooted in a region where wood and clean water and soil were often in short supply, and also an extension of the faith's egalitarian ethics.

"Rich or poor, the body is exposed naked to the rays of the sun and birds of prey," he said. "It's the same."

But after playing its ritual role for centuries, South Asia's vulture population has plunged because of a certain painkiller used on the cattle they eat. India moved to ban the drug, diclofenac, for animals this year.

Nick Lindsay, head of the arm of the Zoological Society of London that runs a vulture conservation centre in northern India, notes the diclofenac problem is unique to the region because it is home to tens of millions of cows living full lives and thus requiring treatment in their old age.

"That's because of their sacred status. So you've got a whole load of cattle and therefore many more carcasses than if the cattle had been used for purely commercial farming," he said.

Other Solutions Are Theologically Wrong

Without vultures, Mumbai's dakhma now relies on solar concentrators to magnify the sun's effect on the bodies, which Mistree sees as a problem.

"Who are they fooling? They're actually burning the body," he said. "It's like a cheap fix, but theologically totally wrong... The body is totally charred, like a burns victim. It's terrible."

Shroff dismisses this and argues the blackening effects of exposure on a body are similar. He also said something had to be done quickly because the punchayet faced threats of lawsuits from deep-pocketed local residents complaining about the smell.

"We are not looking at it as scholars," he said. "We have to look at it from an administration, managerial, hygienic point of view. We have to look at the entire community, not just the Parsis."

The dakhma had also briefly tried using chemicals, but pall bearers refused to take part because of the "ankle-deep sludge" left behind, punchayet trustee Dinshaw Tamboly said.

Supporters say no more than 75 [vultures] would be needed to consume the average three Parsis who die every day..., while skeptics say that figure is 100 vultures short.

Another proposal, backed by environmentalists and traditionalists alike, was for a huge aviary around the dakhma where vultures could be bred.

Supporters say no more than 75 captive birds would be needed to consume the average three Parsis who die every day in Mumbai, while skeptics say that figure is 100 vultures short.

The punchayet says the aviary idea remains on a back burner, but insists it has little money to support it given its obligations to subsidize Mumbai's Parsis from cradle to grave.

"Our priority is towards the living, not towards the dead," Tamboly said.

The punchayet sponsors a fertility programme and increases subsidies as families grow, for the community faces its own survival battle.

Almost one in three are older than 60 and, in a problem familiar in the West, their well-educated offspring have fewer children and get married later, if at all.

The women often marry non-Parsis, and Mistree worries about reformists who want to accept their offspring into the fold, so he set up the World Association of Parsi Irani Zoroastrians to rival the more liberal world body.

"If ethnicity goes, the identity goes," he said. "And if the identity goes, we believe our religion will die."

12

Plastination Is an Appropriate Way to Dispose of the Dead

Tony Walter

Tony Walter is professor of death studies and the director of a graduate program in death and society at the University of Bath, in Bath, England.

Plastination, a technique developed by German anatomist Gunther von Hagens wherein a human corpse can be preserved for millennia, is a new form of body disposal. In this technique, bodies are treated with resin so that they can be exhibited in a vertical position, making them more valuable for educational purposes. A popular exhibition of plastinated bodies, Body Worlds, *has toured Europe and the United States. Viewers accepted both the process and method of disposition. In addition, most people who donated their bodies for plastination find the technique to be a respectful and dignified way to dispose of their bodies.*

The methods by which human bodies may be respectfully disposed of are limited, and each society strictly regulates which methods are acceptable. When a new method is introduced, it can be controversial. An example is the replacement of endocannibalism by burial in the Amazonian society researched by Conklin (2001). In the Western context, examples include the introduction of anatomical dissection from the sixteenth century onwards, discussions in the 1870s to intro-

Tony Walter, "Plastination for Display: A New Way to Dispose of the Dead," *Journal of the Royal Anthropological Institute*, vol. 10, no. 3, September 2004, pp. 603–627. Copyright © Royal Anthropological Institute 2004. Reproduced by permission of Blackwell Publishers and the author.

duce cremation to a number of Western countries for the first time in nearly two millennia, and media coverage in the late twentieth century of the prohibitively expensive process of cryonic freezing (which is in any case not a final disposal, or so hope those who have paid to have their bodies preserved in this way). All proved controversial.

Plastination

Another recent innovation is plastination. Whereas in a number of societies disposed-of bodies are visible and/or retrievable, for example through secondary burial or mummification, in most modern Western societies the human form is usually rendered invisible within coffin or casket and then destroyed by burial or cremation. Plastinated bodies, though, are permanent, and presented for public display. From the mid-1990s till the time of writing (April 2004) 14 million people in nine countries have visited *Körperwelten/Body Worlds*, a travelling exhibition of plastinated bodies, and over 5,000 people have signed forms, available at the exhibition, donating their bodies for plastination.

Does the donor's sacrifice of their corpse for [plastination and] public display perhaps create immortality for them and/or enlightenment for exhibition visitors?

While many journalistic articles and a few scholarly works have commented on this popular and controversial exhibition, they have not focused on the fact that it constitutes a new way to dispose of the dead. In Britain, there are very few legal prohibitions concerning the mode of dealing with dead bodies. The law can be more restrictive elsewhere: in some parts of Europe, for example, human remains—including cremated remains—must be buried. But whatever the legal position, how does the public feel about disposal by plastination? . . .

A number of early anthropologists . . . highlighted the fear of the dead, whether of body or ghost. Do *Body Worlds* visitors fear, loathe, find disgusting, or otherwise react with visceral negativity to the remains on display? . . . What kind of symbolic transformation of the corpse is achieved by plastination and subsequent display?. . . Does the donor's sacrifice of their corpse for public display perhaps create immortality for them, and/or enlightenment for exhibition visitors?

Plastination and the Study of Anatomy

I suggest that [Anthropologist R.] Hertz's (1960) notion of wet and dry burial is particularly informative. In the double funerals that Hertz analysed, the wet burial ritually disposes of the fresh corpse; there is then an intermediary period in which the decomposition of the body is mirrored by the passage of the soul and the ritual actions of mourners; this is ended by the dry funeral, in which the dry remains are recovered, and ritually re-disposed of in a permanent location. In the Hertzian scheme, wet corpses are objects of mourning; dry remains are not. Plastination transforms a flesh corpse to be mourned into dry remains that may be exhibited as objects of curiosity and/or scientific education, turning a ritual (for there are no funerals, wet or dry) into a technical process, the stated aim being not the destiny of the soul but the extension of anatomical education to a lay audience.

The study of anatomy was a key element of early modern science. It literally opened up the mysteries of the body's interior, in the way that geology came to open up the earth's interior and astronomy the hidden recesses of the universe. From the sixteenth to eighteenth centuries, public dissections were well attended, but had to be conducted quickly, so were typically restricted to the winter months, and the supply of bodies was often problematic. From the early eighteenth century, it became possible to preserve organs in solution, enabling their display in jars. Corrosion-casting, in which arteries and veins are injected with resin and then the other tissue corroded away to reveal the intricate structure of the blood vessels, has been used for more than two centuries, but dry preservation of other soft tissue proved elusive. Consequently, by the eighteenth century, skilfully made wax anatomical models were being produced. From the nineteenth century, formalin enabled better preservation both of organs in solution, and of entire corpses for prolonged dissection by individual students.

Plastinated specimens are expected to remain stable for at least four thousand years.

Anatomy museums have been open to the general public in Italy, Germany, Austria, and Switzerland through to the present day, but in the UK since the mid-nineteenth century such museums have been restricted to doctors and medical students, with the exception of London's Hunterian Museum of comparative anatomy. By the mid-twentieth century, viewing anatomized human remains in continental museums, or not being able to view them in British museums, was of no great interest to the general public, journalists, or cultural critics.

Gunther von Hagens and *Body Worlds*

The possibilities of preservation and of display, and of public interest, increased dramatically in the work of the medically trained German anatomist Gunther von Hagens. From the 1970s, von Hagens, the creator of *Body Worlds*, developed plastination, a process that replaces the body's 70 per cent water with a resin that hardens not only blood vessels but also any tissue, so that the body, or any combination of body parts, can be displayed in its normal vertical position. He sold both resin and completed plastinates to medical schools, but from 1996 he also mounted the *Körperwelten/Body Worlds* public exhibition, which was shown in Japan, Germany, Austria, Switzerland, Belgium, Britain, South Korea, Taiwan, and Singapore, with an annual turnover of 20 million euros, until in April 2004, following ongoing public hostility in von Hagens' home country, Germany, from sections of the press, academia, local government, and other quarters, plans were announced to locate the exhibition permanently in the USA. Von Hagens' organization is partly based in Heidelberg, where he originally trained, while the production of plastinates has been transferred to [the city of] Dalian in China, where cheap and highly skilled technicians, seventy of whom are medically trained, produce per annum a thousand individual specimens (e.g. arm or leg slices, individual organs) and fifteen whole body specimens, each of which takes 1,500 skilled person-hours to create. Altogether, the organization has about four hundred employees.

Display Innovations

Body Worlds makes at least four significant innovations. First, spatial relationships between organs, and their position within the body, can now be shown, reflecting the individuality of actual human anatomy rather than the idealized average displayed by textbook drawings, models, and computer simulations. Secondly, the exhibits need not be encased in liquid in glass jars, in turn protected within glass cases: whole-body plastinates can stand erect in the same space inhabited by the viewer. Thirdly, whereas previously people could donate their bodies for dissection (with whatever is left over eventually being buried or cremated), now people can donate their body for plastination, in the knowledge that this will be the body's final disposal. Plastinated specimens are expected to remain stable for at least four thousand years.

Fourth, von Hagens is committed to bringing anatomy out of the cabinet and into public view. His mission is to democratize anatomy, so that everyone—not just medics—can learn about their own bodies through studying the dead. To this end, he brings his flair for showmanship, though some critics hold that this undermines the integrity of his educational purpose. Some of the plastinates are exhibited in physical poses (such as running or swimming), while others are shown in more clearly social poses (as a basketball player, cyclist, swordsman, or chess player). Von Hagens has given his donors a new identity: the cyclist may never have known how to cycle, the swimmer may not have been able to swim, the basketball player may never have played basketball. Von Hagens himself has compared this to plastic surgery, and to the posthumous name that Buddhist monks in Japan give the deceased. Some of these posthumous identities echo those in anatomical drawings of the sixteenth to eighteenth centuries, blow-ups of which adorn the exhibition walls. . . .

Some donors are attracted by plastination because it avoids the messiness of burial and the banality of cremation.

Though von Hagens runs a successful medium-size international business without public subsidy or family endowment, I see little evidence for the charge often made by critics that he is motivated by profit. He ploughs profits back into the business, sleeps very little, and works the rest of the time. He is a charismatic leader who picks staff on ability and loyalty rather than qualifications, and several family members are also involved in the business. Always innovating, he surrounds himself with creative people; unconcerned about official permissions or fashions in museum display, he implements new ideas immediately and hopes for the best. His lack of respect for government-imposed rules and regulations that might limit his mission may stem from his upbringing, early studies, and imprisonment in the former East Germany. He cares little about respectability in the eyes of the establishment, is happiest when *Body Worlds* attracts people from backgrounds other than the museum-visiting middle classes, and knows that controversy is his best marketing tool.

Since the mid-nineteenth century, museums and other educational establishments have sought, successfully, to differentiate themselves from shows and fairgrounds. It is not surprising, then, that von Hagens' eccentric mix of showmanship and scientific instruction—though acceptable to most visitors—can disturb professional critics. He is also sometimes thought of as a postmodernist deliberately playing with ambiguity, but in my view he is someone who defies conventional categories; indeed I believe that he is too driven by his professed mission to teach people about their bodies to concern himself with such matters. Though ultimately he positions *Body Worlds* as education rather than entertainment, as science rather than art, the exhibition forces many visitors to rethink such categories. Von Hagens is constantly pushing the boundaries of the acceptable, for example in his conducting a public autopsy in London in November 2002, prompting the public to reveal what it will or will not accept in relation to the dead. . . .

What Do Donors Think?

A full examination of plastination as a new alternative to burial, cremation, or ordinary anatomical dissection requires an analysis of the language used by donors. Why do they donate? What meaning does it hold for them? . . . First, of the four donors I interviewed, none had any qualms about the poses or uses to which their plastinated bodies would be put; even though some visitors may find certain poses degrading to the dead, it would seem very unlikely that any donors, having themselves visited the exhibition, would feel the same way.

Secondly, some donors are attracted by plastination because it avoids the messiness of burial and the banality of cremation. A British journalist who interviewed a number of donors wrote that each "seems to have chosen plastination as a solution to the problem of how their own deaths should be dealt with. It also represents a handy antidote to the mournful attitude to death prescribed by the Victorians and with which we still live." For donors quoted in the donation information pack, plastination has an elegance that burial and cremation cannot match:

> There is a lot of talk about "dying with dignity" but little about treating dead bodies in a dignified manner. The limited possibilities—to be either burned or to rot in earth—always seemed degrading to me and were problematic (female, born 1953).

> My soul will know that its body is in good hands. I will keep my eye on it. Thank you very much for this new possibility. To bring last things to an end so elegantly (male, born 1962).

One's body may be perceived to be not only in good hands, but in better hands than in life:

> With regard to my body, I really have not treated it well after decades of bulimia. . . I will make this body available to you, my body which probably will be difficult to handle for me for the rest of my life (female, born 1956).

People in Britain often choose cremation over burial because they perceive it as cleaner, more hygienic, more dignified (Walter 1990); plastination takes this a step further. In fact, given the overall messiness of life on earth, one 14-year-old girl writes in the guestbook of plastination as

> wonderful and a class act—five stars! I hope one day I'll be a dead mummy for display before we all get killed by global warming, species of animals die, meteors hit earth, flooding, radiation, deserts spreading, no water.

Visitors Approve of Plastination

Mummification for eternity (or at least millennia) is now a practical possibility for anyone willing to pay for their corpse's shipment to the Institute of Plastination in China, at a price comparable to that of a conventional funeral.

Body Worlds *also shows a degree of artistic display and showmanship redolent of the Catholic mummies of Italy.*

In northwestern Europe, where mummification is not practised, a corpse with soft tissue smells and rots, and is, in Hertz's terminology, wet; dry remains are composed of bone or ash. *Body Worlds*, by displaying soft tissue that is dry, does not smell, and is stable, confuses such assumptions about wet and dry. This is likely to be particularly troublesome in the advertising pictures, whose viewers may well imagine smell and rot. What is surprising, therefore, is the speed with which plastination is accepted by the majority of *Body Worlds* visitors. To quote one advertising leaflet, "Laypersons have reacted in a completely different way to the exhibition than was predicted by experts." If visitors overwhelmingly approve of the process of plastination, subject to the deceased's previous consent, it is because they accept that these objects were once corpses, but are no longer; they have been transformed into dry remains, into scientific exhibits, losing their original personhood.

But *Body Worlds* also shows a degree of artistic display and showmanship redolent of the Catholic mummies of Italy, its baroque extravaganza contrasting with the minimalist funeral cultures of late twentieth-century northern Europe. And it is here that the problems come, in certain forms of display and surface features, both of which re-personalize the exhibits. These features divide visitors. The greater the artistic licence in the poses, the less clinical the exhibits become, and the less legitimate they become, for some visitors.

A new way to dispose of human corpses—plastination for display—has indeed arrived. In the long run, though, precisely because plastination is so permanent, demand for donors may prove limited. Once the number of medical schools replacing traditional anatomical donation with plastination has plateaued, and once von Hagens has achieved his aim of a permanent public exhibition on every continent, some of those signing donation forms today may, when they decease, find their services no longer required. The young visitor who wrote, "I hope one day I'll be a dead mummy for display" had perhaps better not live too long.

Organizations to Contact

The editors have compiled the following list of organizations concerned with the issues debated in this book. The descriptions are derived from materials provided by the organizations. All have publications or information available for interested readers. The list was compiled on the date of publication of the present volume; the information provided here may change. Be aware that many organizations take several weeks or longer to respond to inquiries, so allow as much time as possible.

AARP
601 E. Street, NW, Washington, DC   20049
(888) 687-2277
Web site: www.aarp.org

AARP is a membership organization for people fifty years of age and older. It provides extensive funeral-related information on its Web site as well as information about loss and grief.

Buddha Dharma Education Association
78 Bentley Road, Tullera, NSW   2480
   Australia
612-6628-2426
E-mail: bdea@buddhanet.net
Web site: www.buddhanet.net

The Buddha Dharma Education Association provides information about the many different schools of Buddhist thought, primarily through its Web site. There is significant information on the site regarding Buddhist death rituals as well as additional resources and links to other sites.

Cremation Association of North America (CANA)
401 North Michigan Avenue, Chicago, IL   60611
(312) 245-1077

E-mail: cana@smithbucklin.com
Web site: www.cremationassociation.org

CANA is an association of crematories, cemeteries, and funeral homes offering cremation. It also publishes the *Cremationist* magazine. The organization's Web site contains articles about cremation, surveys of North American attitudes toward cremation, and discussions of the environmental issues of cremation.

Crossings: Caring for Our Own at Death
7108 Holly Avenue, Takoma Park, MD   20912
(301) 523-3033
E-mail: crossingcare@earthlink.net
Web site: www.crossings.net

Crossings is a nonprofit organization dedicated to helping people learn about caring for their own dead. The organization sponsors workshops and maintains a helpful Web site where students will find inspirational messages, suggestions for services, links to other Web sites, and a frequently-asked-questions page.

Eternal Reefs
P.O. Box 2473, Decatur, GA   30031
(888) 423-7333
E-mail: info@eternalreefs
Web site: www.eternalreefs.com

Eternal Reefs is a business that helps customers arrange for the final disposition of the remains of cremated bodies in an artificial, undersea reef. The Web site contains information regarding the service as well as additional resources about undersea reefs.

U.S. Federal Trade Commission
(800) 877-FTC-HELP
Web site: www.ftc.gov

The Federal Trade Commission is the United States governmental agency charged with protecting the consumer from fraud and illegal business practices. Its Web site includes, among other helpful information, *Funerals: A Consumer Guide*. This thirty-page downloadable booklet covers virtually every aspect of the disposal of the dead.

Final Passages
P.O. Box 1721, Sebastopol, CA   95473
(707) 824-0268
E-mail: info@finalpassages.org
Web site: finalpassages.org

Final Passages is an organization that provides death midwifery assistance. Its Web site provides articles and resources concerning the home burial and do-it-yourself funeral movement.

Funeral Consumers Alliance
33 Patchen Road, South Burlington, VT   05403
(802) 865-8300
Web site: www.funerals.org

The Funeral Consumers Alliance is a nonprofit organization that advises consumers on funerary practices and options. It provides information on legal matters concerning the disposal of the dead as well as practical suggestions for families and individuals about how to care for their dead. Through its Web site, the organization offers many helpful brochures and pamphlets that can be downloaded and printed. In addition, the organization publishes a quarterly newsletter.

Kavod v'Nichum
8112 Sea Water Path, Columbia, MD   21045
(410) 733-3700
E-mail: zinner@jewish-funerals.org
Web site: www.jewish-funerals.org

Kavod v'Nichum, which means "honor and comfort," is an organization advocating the growth of the Chevra Kadisha, a

Jewish burial society. The group's Web site is a source of information regarding traditional Jewish death practices. There are many articles, links, and resources available on the site.

Green Burial Council
8 Estacada Court, Santa Fe, NM   87508
(888) 966-3330
Web site: www.greenburialcouncil.org

Green Burial Council is a nonprofit organization that encourages environmentally sound death care. The organization encourages the acquisition, restoration, and stewardship of land, and provides significant information for consumers who need help in finding a "green" cemetery or other funerary services. The Web site includes links to other sites, articles, and information about the concept of green burial.

International Cemetery, Cremation, and Funeral Association (ICCFA)
107 Carpenter Drive, Sterling, VA   20164
(703) 391-8400
Web site: www.icfa.org

The ICCFA is an advocacy group that, according to its Web site, promotes "consumer choices, prearrangement, and open competition" in funeral arrangements. The Web site has many resources and links, including a blog. The site also includes a virtual reading room with articles and additional information.

Islamic Society of North America (ISNA)
P.O. Box 38, Plainfield, IN   46168
(317) 839-8157
Web site: www.isna.net

The ISNA is an organization dedicated to spreading information about Islam and to improve the quality of Muslim life in North America. The organization publishes a newsletter and provides information on its Web site about Islamic death practices.

Memorial Ecosystems
111 West Main Street, Westminster, SC   29693
(864) 647-7798
E-mail: Kimberley@memorialecosystems.com
Web site: www.memorialecosystems.com

Memorial Ecosystems is a company specializing in conservation burial. Ramsey Creek Preserve, one of the first green burial sites in the United States, is managed by this company. The Web site contains information regarding conservation burial, including news articles, frequently asked questions, and links to other resources.

National Funeral Directors Association (NFDA)
13625 Bishop's Drive, Brookfield, WI   53005
(800) 228-6332
Web site: www.nfda.org

NFDA is a professional association of American funeral directors. Its Web site includes significant information for consumers concerning funeral practices, options, and price ranges.

Bibliography

Books

Sandra Gilbert, *Modern Dying and the Ways We Grieve*. New York: Norton, 2006.

Gunther von Hagens and Angelina Whalley, *Gunther von Hagens' Body Worlds: The Anatomical Exhibition of Real Human Bodies*. Exhibition Catalog, translated by F. Kelly, Heidelberg, Germany: Arts and Sciences, and Institute for Plastination, 2005.

Mark Harris, *Grave Matters: A Journey Through the Modern Funeral Industry to a Natural Way of Burial*. New York: Scribner, 2007.

Gary Laderman, *Rest In Peace: A Cultural History of Death and the Funeral Home in Twentieth-Century America*. New York: Oxford University Press, 2003.

Mary Roach, *Stiff: The Curious Lives of Human Cadavers*. New York: Norton, 2003.

Michael Sledge, *Soldier Dead: How We Recover, Identify, Bury, and Honor Our Military Fallen*. New York: Columbia University Press, 2005.

Periodicals

Ramola Talwar Badam, "Photos of Corpses Spark Furor in India," *Chicago Sun-Times*, September 8, 2006.

Carolyn Banks, "Beyond the Urn: Getting Creative with Cremains," *LifeTimes*, July 2006.

Barbara Basler, "Green Graveyards: A Natural Way to Go," *AARP Bulletin*, July/August 2004.

Jariel Bortnik, "Cremation Growing in Popularity," *Gainesville* (Fla.) *Sun*, December 10, 2007.

Jaye Christensen, "The Eco Way to Go," *Common Ground*, April 2007.

Stephen F. Christy, Jr., "The Final Stop for Land Trusts," *The Land Trust Alliance Exchange*, Spring 2007.

Chelsea Conaboy, "Business Proposes Alternative to Cremation: Process Dissolves the Body in Water, Alkali," *Concord* (N.H.) *Monitor*, August 27, 2007.

Gabrielle Coppola, "Monks Go Green," *Business Week*, October 23, 2007.

Douglas Davies, "The Invisibles: We Can Choose to Shun Death, But It's a Choice That Comes with Consequences," *New Scientist*, October 13, 2007.

Joe Eaton, "Silent Towers, Empty Skies," *Earth Island Journal*, Winter 2004.

Sylvia Fraser, "Things To Do in Toronto When You're Dead," *Toronto Life*, December 2004.

Jeremy Gantz, "Religious Groups Disagree on Medical Donations," *Medill Reports*, May 24, 2007. http://news.medill.northwestern.edu/chicago.

Christine Gordillo, "Law Allows Individuals to Pick Point Person for Final Arrangements," *Crain's Cleveland Business*, August 2007.

Anthony Gottschlich, "Do-It-Yourself Funeral Is One Available Option," *Dayton* (Ohio) *Daily News*, June 5, 2007.

David E. Harrington and Edward A. Sayre, "Paying for Bodies, But Not for Organs," *Regulation*, Winter 2006–2007.

Monica Hatcher, "Are We Becoming a Cremation Nation?" *Miami Herald*, February 6, 2006.

Deborah Hirsch, "Faiths Offer Ways to Mourn," *News & Observer* (N.C.), June 15, 2007.

Peter Holderness, "A Movement for Green Life After Death," *Medill Reports*, November 1, 2007. http://news.medill.northwestern.edu/chicago.

Kerry Howley, "Who Owns Your Body Parts? Everyone's Making Money in the Market for Body Tissue—Except the Donors," *Reason*, March 2007.

Julia McKinnell, "No Happy Returns: Burials at Sea May Be Environmentally Friendly, But What If . . . ," *Maclean's*, September 10, 2007.

Gilbert Meilaender, "Broken Bodies Redeemed: Bioethics and the Troublesome Union of Body and Soul." *Touchstone*, January/February 2007.

Charleen M. Moore and C. Mackenzie Brown, "Experiencing *Body Worlds*: Voyeurism, Education, or Enlightenment?" *Journal of Medical Humanities*, 2007.

Oliver Morgan, et al., "Mass Fatality Management Following the South Asian Tsunami Disaster: Case Studies in Thailand, Indonesia, and Sri Lanka," *PloS Medicine*, Fall 2006.

Vanessa Murray, "Pushing Up Daisies," *Nova*, June 2006.

Thomas A. Parmalee, "Biocides Directive Causes a Storm of Controversy," *American Funeral Director*, March 2007.

Paul Rahill, "Mercury and Cremation: Issues Revisited," *Cremationist*, August/September/October 2004.

Dawn Rolke with Lee Moats, "The Rituals and Politics of Death," *Briarpatch*, April 2004.

Nancy Rommelmann, "Crying and Digging," *Los Angeles Times*, February 6, 2005.

Tiffany Sharples, "Unlikely Teachers: The Enduring Role of Cadavers in Educating Future Doctors," *Medill Reports*, May 18, 2007. http://news.medill.northwestern.edu/chicago.

Bill Strubbe, "Death Midwifery and the Home Funeral Revolution," *Common Ground*, April 2007.

Malcolm Tait, "Towers of Silence," *The Ecologist*, October 2004.

Index

A

AARP, 105
Accidental death, 56
Agency for Toxic Substance and Disease Registry, 31, 32–33
Aging, 60–61
Alcohol, 56–57
Allnutt, Rick, 42–46
Amazonian society, 95
Archaeology, 54–55
Arizona State University, 54
Arsenic, 29–32

B

Bad deaths, 56–57
Black Death, 58
Bodies in Motion and at Rest: On Metaphor and Mortality (Lynch), 75
Body
    body viewing, 37–38
    excarnation ritual and, 85–91
    memorial services and, 79–81
    presence at funeral, 75–84
    resurrection and, 23
    as shell, 77–78
    shipping for green burial, 39
    as temple of Holy Spirit, 26
    See also Plastination
Body preparation after death
    Buddhism and, 85, 87
    Christianity and, 25–28
    Hinduism and, 12
    Islam and, 15–16
    Judaism and, 16

    Sikhs and, 14
    toxic emissions and, 42–46
Body Worlds (science exhibition), 95, 98–101
Bone Woman (Koff), 64
Book of Common Prayer, 71, 73
Bradshaw, Richard, 69–73
British Broadcasting Corp. (BBC), 44
Bucci, John, 37, 38
Buddha Dharma Education Association, 105
Buddhism
    beliefs, 18, 88–89
    excarnation death ritual, 85–91
    kamma and, 18
    nirvana and, 18
    timing of funerary rituals, 18–19
Bulsara, Farrokh, 91
Burial, Hinduism and, 13

C

Callwood, June, 69
Campbell, Billy, 35, 40
Campbell, Kimberley, 36, 40
Canada, 33, 39, 66
Canadian Opera Company, 69–70
Cardboard caskets, 36
Caring for the Dead—Your Final Act of Love (Carlson), 8
Carlson, Lisa, 8
Caskets, 29, 31–32, 36, 38–39, 63, 77
Catholic Church, 23–28

Catholic Order of Christian Funerals (OCF), 24, 26
Cattle, 92
Chevra Kadisha, 8–9
China, 103
Christianity
  beliefs, 19, 23, 24, 26, 77–81
  Catholic Church, 23–28
  cremation and, 20, 23–26
  funerary rituals, 19–20, 63–64, 70–74, 75–84
Christy, Stephen F., 7, 8
Civil War, embalming and, 7, 32
Coal, 43, 44
Coffins, 29, 31–32, 36, 38–39, 63, 77
Colorado, 42–46
Colorado State University, 45
Communication with dead, 54
Correll, DeeDee, 42
Costs of funerals
  average cost, 41
  green burial, 40–41
Council for Geoscience, 30
Cremation
  body preparation for, 12, 14
  Christianity and, 20, 23–26
  as environmentally friendly, 48–49
  Hinduism and, 11–13
  introduction of, 96
  Intuitive Logic Control (ILC), 51–52
  Islam and, 11
  Judaism and, 11, 17
  opacity controls and, 50–51
  oxygen control and, 52
  reasons for choice of, 102
  Sikhs and, 11, 14–15
  temperature control and, 49–50
    toxic emissions and, 42–46, 49–50, 52
Cremation Association of North America (CANA), 44, 45, 105–106
Creosote, 33
Crossings: Caring for Our Own at Death (organization), 106
Cryonic freezing, 96

D

Davies, Robertson, 73
Death
  bad death, 56–58
  fear of, 19, 55, 56, 58, 78, 97
  gerophobia and, 61
  good death, 76–77
  as inconvenience, 59–60
  obituaries and, 66–68
  as obscured, 66
  rites of passage and, 58–59
Diana, Princess, 72
Diclofenac, 92
Donne, John, 65, 74
Doyle, John, 69, 74
Dry burials, 97, 103

E

Embalming
  arsenic and, 29–32
  Civil War and, 7, 32
  creosote and, 33
  formaldehyde and, 29–33
  mercury and, 33
  as optional, 38
  pollution of groundwater and, 29–34
Endocannibalism, 95
Environmental Protection Agency, U.S. (EPA), 30, 32, 33, 43–45, 47, 49

Eternal Reefs, 106
Eulogies, 69–70
Excarnation, 85–91

F

Fear of death, 56
Final Passages (organization), 107
Forever Fernwood (cemetery), 41
Formaldehyde, 29–34
Formalin, 98
Fotheringham, Allan, 71–72
Fraser, John, 65–74
Fulton, Richard D.L., 29–34
Funeral Consumers Alliance, 107
Funerals
    bad deaths and, 56–58
    body present at, 75–84
    Christian funerary rituals,
        19–20
    contemporary funeral, 63–64,
        70–74, 75–84
    costs of, 25, 30–31, 40–41, 60,
        66, 77–79
    dry funerals, 97, 103
    eulogies, 69–70
    generational differences in
        attitude about, 60–61
    good funerals, 77
    Hindu funerary rituals, 12–13
    history of, 54–55
    as honor for dead, 65–74
    Islamic funerary rituals, 15–16
    Jewish funerary rituals, 16–18
    memorial services, 79–81
    for nonreligious, 20–22, 61–62
    obituaries and, 66–68
    purpose of, 53–64
    rite-of-passage theory and,
        58–59
    Sikh funerary rituals, 14–15
    timing of funerary rituals, 16
    virtual funerals, 63

wet burials, 97, 103
    See also Green burial; Home
        burial movement

G

Ganges River, 12, 13
George, Francis, archbishop of
    Chicago, 26–27
Gerophobia, 61
Global warming, 47–48
Globe and Mail (Canadian
    newspaper), 66, 69
God, 14–17, 19, 26, 48, 55, 73,
    78–79
Grave digging, 37–38
*Grave Matters: A Journey Through
    the Modern Funeral Industry to a
    Natural Way of Burial* (Harris),
    8, 38
Green burial
    body viewing and, 37–38
    coffin types used, 36, 63
    costs of, 40–41
    downside of, 37–38
    grave markets, 36
    land conservation and, 35–36,
        40
    popularity of, 37
    practices of, 8, 35
    See also Home burial move-
        ment
Green Burial Council, 37, 39, 108
Greensprings cemetery, New York,
    38, 41

H

Harris, Mark, 8, 38–40
Haunting, 58
Hawaii, 44
Herbert, George, 65

Hinduism
    beliefs, 11–12
    body preparation for cremation, 12
    burial of young children, 13
    cremation and, 7, 11–13
Holderness, Peter, 8
Home burial movement, 8–10
    See also Green burial
Homicide, 56
Humanism, 20–22
Hunterian Museum of London, 98

I

Imam, 15
India, 90–94
Institute of Plastination in China, 103
International Cemetery, Cremation, and Funeral Association (ICCFA), 108
Internet, 63
Intuitive Logic Control (ILC), 51–52
Islam
    beliefs, 15
    body preparation after death, 15–16
    cremation and, 11
    Imam, 15
    Qu'ran, 15
Islamic Society of North America (ISNA), 108

J

Jesus, 81
Joseph of Arimathea, 81
Judaism
    beliefs, 16
    body preparation after death, 16
    burial societies, 8–9
    cremation and, 11, 17
    embalming prohibited, 38
    funeral traditions, 16–18
    rabbis, 17
    timing of funerary rituals, 16

K

Kamma, 18
Karma, 11–12
Kastenbaum, Robert, 53–64
Kavod v'Nichum, 107–108
Koff, Clea, 64
Konefes, John L., 31–32
Kozak, David, 57

L

Laribee, Rachel, 85–89
Lindsay, Nick, 92
Loved One (Waugh), 67
Lynch, Dennis, 45
Lynch, Thomas, 75–84
Lyons, 10

M

Maine, 44
Marriage, 92
Marty, John, 44
Maryland Department of the Environment, 33
Mass graves, 58–59, 64
McCall, Christina, 70–73
McGee, Michael K., 31–32
McMillan, Mark, 43, 45
Memorial Ecosystems, 109
Memorial services, 79–81
Mercury, 33, 42–43
Mercury, Freddie, 91
Methyl alcohol, 31

Minnesota, 44

Mistree, Khojeste, 91–94

Movement for Green Life After Death (Holderness), 8

N

National Funeral Directors Association (NFDA), 41, 109

Nevada, 44

Newman, Peter C., 72–73

Nicodemus, 81

Nirvana, 18

O

Obituaries, 66–68

Old Cemeteries, Arsenic, and Health Safety (Konefes and McGee), 31

P

Parsis, 90–94

Paul, Saint, 79

Perez-Sullivan, Margot, 44

Pilate, 81

Plastination
    anatomical study and, 97–98, 101–104
    body display and, 96
    Body Worlds and, 98–101
    reaction to, 97, 99, 102–103
    See also Body

Power plants, 43, 44

Project Compassion, 75

Q

Qu'ran, 15

R

Rabbis, 17

Rahill, Paul F., 47–52

Ramsey Creek Preserve, South Carolina, 35–36, 39, 41

Reddall, Braden, 90–94

Reincarnation, 88–89

Resurrection, 23

Rituals and Politics of Death (Rolke), 7

Rolke, Dawn, 7

Rwanda, 64

Ryan, Doug, 46

S

Schade, Michael, 69–70, 74

Scharnberg, Kristen, 35–41

Schee, Joe, 37

September 11 terrorist attack, 58–59

Shroff, Minoo, 92–93

Sikhs
    beliefs, 14
    body preparation for cremation, 14
    cremation and, 11, 14–15

Sky burial, 85–89

Soul, 78–79

South Africa, 33

Spencer, Earl, 72

Suicide, 56

Survivor stress, 58

T

Tamboly, Dinshaw, 93

Tata, J.N., 91

Teeth, 42–46

Teresa, St. of Avila, 26–27

Tibet, 85–89

Tohono O'odham, 56–57

Trobriand Islanders, 56

U

Undertaking: Life Studies in the Dismal Trade (Lynch), 75
United Kingdom, 33, 44, 95
University of Bath (England), 95
U.S. Environmental Protection Agency (EPA), 30, 32, 33, 43–45, 47, 49
U.S. Federal Trade Commission, 106–107

V

Valhalla, 66
Virtual funerals, 63
Vishnu, 12

Von Hagens, Gunther, 95, 98–101
Vultures, 87–88, 90–94

W

Walter, Tony, 95–104
Wet burials, 97, 103
Winfrey, Oprah, 72
World Association of Parsi Irani Zoroastrians, 94
World Trade Center, 58–59

Z

Zoological Society of London, 92
Zoroastrianism, 90–94